DECANTING

Other Books by STUART FRIEBERT

POETRY

Dreaming of Floods
Near Occasions of Sin
Calming Down
Speak Mouth to Mouth
Up in Bed
Floating Heart
Stories My Father Can Tell
On the Bottom
Uncertain Health
Kein Trinkwasser
The Darmstadt Orchids
Die Prokuristen kommen
Funeral Pie
Nicht Hinauslehnen

PROSE

Der Gast, und sei er noch so schlecht

TRANSLATIONS

Günter Eich: *Valuable Nail: Selected Poems* (with David Walker & David Young)
Karl Krolow: *On Account Of: Selected Poems*
Miroslav Holub: *Sagittal Section: Selected Poems* (with Dana Habova)
Giovanni Raboni: *The Coldest Year of Grace: Selected Poems* (with Vinio Rossi)
Marin Sorescu: *Hands Behind My Back: Selected Poems* (with Gabriela Dragnea &
    Adriana Varga)
Karl Krolow: *What'll We Do With This Life?: Selected Poems*
Judita Vaiciunaite: *Fire, Put Put By Fire: Selected Poems* (with Viktoria Skrupskelis)
Sylva Fischerova: *The Swing in the Middle of Chaos: Selected Poems* (with the author)
Sylva Fischerova: *Stomach of the Soul: Selected Poems* (with the author & A.J. Hauner)
Karl Krolow: *Puppets in the Wind: Selected Poems*
Kuno Raeber: *Be Quiet*
Kuno Raeber: *Watch Out*
Kuno Raeber: *Votives: Selected Poems* (with Christiane Wyrwa)

ANTHOLOGIES

A Field Guide to Contemporary Poetry & Poetics (with David Young; 2nd edition with
    David Young & David Walker)
The Longman Anthology of Contemporary Poetry (1st & 2nd editions with David Young)
Models of the Universe: An Anthology of the Prose Poem (with David Young)

TEXTBOOK

Max Frisch: *Als der Krieg zu Ende war*

DECANTING

Selected & New Poems · 1967 - 2017

Stuart Friebert

LOST HORSE PRESS
Sandpoint, Idaho

ACKNOWLEDGMENTS

Most of the poems in this collection originally appeared in the following works, some with slightly different titles and altered texts:

Calming Down (Triskelion Press, 1970)
Dreaming of Floods (Vanderbilt University Press, 1969)
Floating Heart (Pinyon Publishing, 2014)
Funeral Pie (Four Way Books, 1996)
Near Occasions of Sin (dOOm-AH Books, 2004)
On the Bottom (Iris Press, 2015)
Speak Mouth to Mouth (David Robert Books, 2009)
Stories My Father Can Tell (Pocket Pal Press, 1975)
The Darmstadt Orchids (BkMk Press: University of Missouri-Kansas City, 1992)
Uncertain Health (Woolmer/Brotherson, LTD, 1979)
Up in Bed (Cleveland State University Press, 1974)

Most of the "new" poems previously appeared in the following journals:

Offcourse
Plume
Plume Anthology
Red Wheelbarrow

Cover Art: Mel McCudden
Author Photo: Cindy Sherman.
Book & Cover Design: Christine Holbert.

FIRST EDITION

This and other LOST HORSE PRESS titles may be viewed online at www.losthorsepress.org.

LIBRARY OF CONGRESS CATALOGING-IN-PUBLICATION DATA

Names: Friebert, Stuart, 1931- author.
Title: Decanting : selected & new poems 1967-2017 / Stuart Friebert.
Description: First edition. | Sandpoint, Idaho : Lost Horse Press, [2017]
Identifiers: LCCN 2016051840 | ISBN 9780996858458 (trade pbk. : alk. paper)
Classification: LCC PS3556.R48 A6 2017 | DDC 811/.54—dc23
LC record available at https://lccn.loc.gov/2016051840

for Diane, Sarah, Stephen, Naomi, Kazu & Thomas (the Wild One)

CONTENTS

from NEAR OCCASIONS OF SIN

from SPEAK MOUTH TO MOUTH

NEW POEMS

from DREAMING OF FLOODS

TAKING THE EXPRESS TO PARIS, TEXAS

The hills wore morning butterflies,
transforming flight. Streams
smelled of wind in the mind.
The sun could rise no higher
and no farther could I fall.
Thoughts ripened, roots
deeper than chokecherry,
near water where dumb fish
spawn in a whirl
of bladeless knives.

Thoughts darken into larks
shredding the butterflies.
Candles come to the branches:
sunlight is sun and light.
The heart sinks deep,

cockles exploding under mind,
bottoms up. The mellow boat's
boards float in the foam. Those
blown sails will never be recovered
in the wind of the prairies.

THE COUNTRY PREACHER

He walked with the weather,
the Bible in the pale meadow of his hand,
preaching to homesteaders, looking at Indians
through their fires watching his eyes
like the roots of a medicine man.

The snake was out of breath, turned
its linen blue eyes at him, a vision
from the Atlantic to the Pacific noon,
reading verses into the snow and sand.

The snake's eyes echoed more light
than the reeds or rocks. In the berry bogs,
it went farther ahead, binding him
in the Canaan twilight of its depth.

Across the valley rotten with summer
the indolent armies wait while
Jackson rides to drink with Lee.

Trees are insects in the orchards.
Two lieutenants stage a race
between Blues and Grays
cheering jumped ditches.

The recruits
pile fence rails and brush
on the swollen carcasses of horses.

The longest of any modern winter.
Snow on a level with you then suddenly
thirty feet deep in the ravines.

She boarded some woodchoppers.
All the water she used washing after them
snow she melted on the catalogue stove.

She remembered some deer
coming through the clogged woods.
They walked into the sharp sun.

The men saw them. The deer
broke the color of the crust
and went too deep.

The woodchoppers,
shoeing the snow,
went for their axes.

KITE FLYING IN JAPAN

Cunningly rigged,
a square, circle, hexagon,
star, fish, dragon, man,
horse, shield all
will fly equally well.

Whole families circle the air,
even crying children and animals
with hands and legs spread thin.

And old men, at night,
retired from life,
fly the loose skies,
lights on their tails
like giant ancestors.

VIRGINIA WOOLF'S DIARIES

In memory of Addison Ward

The hay on the marshes near London
buries the falling light.
Should she think
of death?

A moth steers like a Messerschmitt
shot down on Sunday over the town,
the powder on its wings scrambling.

She walks along the bomb craters
where birds nest. Moths and birds,
she can't stop looking till the moon
comes up like an owl, hooting.

I want to look back at her war,
the lovely free autumn fall
of the fire bombs, belonging.

DIFFUSED ROUTE

after Günter Eich's "Gemischte Route"

Finally the doors are locked,
the gas cocks turned to zero,
ashes in the oven, otherwise
no remains. We can go.

Nothing but ravines, tongues
of snow, where are the roses
of the teacher, the rain animals
through shattered windows, movie
programs through letter slots,
Thursdays.

Where are, after tongues of snow,
after Thursdays, our roads? Waldein
to Hiroshima, between dogs the
steps in a quarry, a stretch
of comfort drawn from barracks,
from rotting grass, rotting ropes.

FISHING OFF FRANCE

Summer 1949

Burly clouds
turn their wheel
into the Channel.

In the red foam
I cast under overcast
for the bodies

I know are there.
Night sweeps
toward the sand,

sits on boggy thrones.
Gleaming faintly, my lure
floats out of the weeds.

HUNTING WITH MY FATHER

The mallards fly, moss
on their foreheads. Fly
across the stubble of
last year's cattails stretched
out over open water.

My father enjoys
the recoil of his 12-gauge,
watches the white smoke
of our guns barking from
the marshes, the moon
in his eyes falling
heavy and slow
into a white nest.

WINGS AND CIRCLES

I lie without life,
die without flesh,

like the feet of mallards
soft and blind.

My body wants the place
where wings and circles are.

BALLAD OF A CHINESE PAINTER

after Albin Zollinger

I paint a lake
and a wooden bridge.
A dwarf moves
through my snow.

I paint a mountain,
a cabin in a valley,
a lamp in the cabin
The dwarf moves closer.

I paint some snow,
steeply up a volcano.
Land like a moon.
Poor dwarf.

In the light,
his wife bathes another.
So he goes on,
erring like snow.

Clouds smother the sky.
Now the snow
becomes a lake,

When I was young
I thought I dreamt
what I painted.

But now the tea swirls in the waiting bowl.
Mountain after mountain,
dwarves in valleys, darkness of lakes.

DREAMING OF FLOODS

for David Young

The river, broad and
black with rain, swept
trees out of the way.

He felt a longing for tea,
the exhaustion
of a Chekhovian man.

For an instant
the early morning light
was green. Men in dark boots

sandbagging the water
were too late. He'd gladly
have gone back to sleep.

Instead he got up, drove
several miles out of town,
simply to die.

I kiss it in the hospital garden.
It is all in white. It
smiles at the grass or a bench.
We walk together to the bridge,
then it runs with all its might
toward the open field.

All afternoon I hunt it
but only find some
beetles fallen on their backs.

from CALMING DOWN

THE STRUGGLE

I trailed the wounded animal
till it dropped out of the woods
to make room for something else.

The hunter who had fired at it
from across the level swamp
ran all the way to meet me.

He was angry, called me names.
We both lost time looking at each other.
Suddenly I turned and fired,

he took a second shot in the same
direction and when I turned to look
he got me from behind, planted

a bullet in my shoulder. I ran
a mile with it in me. Later he
found me, tied a stick to my jaw,

dragged me over the snow
to a deep clearing, knifed
me coolly in the belly,

ripped straight up, cast
one look back
over his shoulder.

LANDSCAPE WITH BRIDGE

From a distance, the bridge calms me,
raises sky from the surface of my blood.

It makes me an offer, is something of a tailor.
I reach it in a bolt, it is a maze of felled trees,

catching the river by its plow and labor.
Dead fish float past. Walleyes smiting

the judge of the past, the water flowing
under one side is not the water flowing

out the other. I hop on a rail, sit on hands.
When frost quits the wood in spring, damage

will be done in body and mind—whole logs
rising, coming from all sides to unite before

the breakdown. Remove self, ransack woods
for new bark and roots, an ancient almanac,

an age of learned ways. Sky water ark animal
fowl humans: nothing is famous for taking care

of what it is. Over sounds and fish I run inland.
With a crude plane, I begin by shaving carved

messages underfoot. After three words, a heart,
I slip through a cryptic inscription, hit coarse water,

the sacraments, become a rod of flesh and iron,
divining, sinking, down down down down done.

It's zero, the furnace is out.
Not the pilot light this time.

We're such damn fools,
waiting for the plumber,

letting the cat out, turning
the oven on, building a fire

with apple wood, grinning,
saying Turkish poems of cold

in the land, swaying but full
of hope on rocking chairs,

the glue holding. Going down
into the body, closing the door,

the beast visible from
the top step, filling with ice.

THE WELLINGTON FAIR

Eager to deserve you,
extending everything,
both feet for instance,
asking for the privilege,
knees sinking, heart popping,
aiming at something illogical,
like the porcelain tub in the
back bathroom, running the
antique water, another skin
is due, marrying you, the
veterinarian's daughter, raising
sick pigs on inherited land,
walking around ditches to
the falling barn, crying
at the Audubon lecture on
Sunday afternoon. Amelia,
it's 1882 and I think through
most of the sermon that night
before I pull the trigger,
topple the kewpie doll, get
one more turn at the fair.

There's a foot of snow
in the Ohio valley,
my family is locked
in the farm, belongs
to this country
against my advice.

Would to God
they would follow me
over the border, leave
most everything here,
fatten our cows there,
waiting for new laws.

The red cedars swell
with night. Underneath,
I smoke and sleep,
the sky's carrying
a bushel of clouds
north.

UP IN BED

For some time, at least. Those days!
Dad the medic in the shack on the street
repair job, uncle Joe doing the WPA mural
just inside the door of the elementary school,
Mom pinching pennies for the next pack
of Luckies, us kids giving away terpin hydrate
from the wreck of our drugstore that cold
morning the pipes burst and Gramma telling
everybody to freeze the cherry tomatoes
till they got to be flaky white spiders . . .
And the parties they threw! They even got
the only other druggist in town to come, who
lived in the huge house next door, delighted
with the arrangement. Jealousy, he'd say,
invents hellos! Up in bed we listened to that,
pressing our ears through the old cedar floor
to the living room talk below, hungry kids
gobbling up dirty stories. Mornings, the dog
catcher came more and more, it seemed
to us on purpose; and the old river drowned
our dog Peggy, because the Fire Chief was
drunk on duty. The hymns were in trouble
weekends, and the collection plates absent
any detail. Nights all eleven cars in town—
You are leaving Lodi, Wisconsin!—must have
been on the icy road to Madison, shuttling
the grownups to the Bijou where Norma
Shearer was describing how a gentleman
came to try his luck with the ladies: Have
I told you I am yours? Well, haven't I?

CEMETERY POEM

1   Kalookie game in the kitchen. Six people,
    related: three couples, scarred round table.

2   Decide to go out to the cemetery
    though it's past midnight.

3   Caretaker's fast asleep, shades down.
    They walk around looking at sacks
    of lime, sundry tools in a shed. See he
    also builds garden swings. Decide
    to order one for sticky summer nights.

4   Get back to cards at 4 A.M. Pinochle.

5   Back out to cemetery.

6   Caretaker shows them choice plots,
    one near the freeway. They count
    the trucks. It occurs to them they
    really care where they'll be buried.

7   Scene shifts to the loveliest spot with
    magnificent sycamore. Cemetery
    has a stack of its postcard they buy.

8   Who gets the tree? First to die, last?

9   By the time the caretaker walks puffing
    down the slope toward them, they are
    turned around, facing him, arm in arm.

CHIMNEY POEM

Keeps saying, come home.
Did not feel inclined to go
that way, sweet bricks of
four old sides taking a vow,
looking out for incidents and
the first chimney in the world
did its work, went to sleep,
the second was my brother
making soldiers of anything
he could find till Dad said
I'll build a house with none,
but bought a weathervane
anyway, tamped the roof
down, and once claimed
he saw a chimney in the sky,
a small one feeding on smoke,
and we thought of heat and
hunger, waited for the light
to settle, climbed it slowly
scraping feet as we went,
kicking the mortar back
till the chimney bellowed:
I will not serve! I will not make
peace with an enemy so easily.

ISN'T IT TRUE

For a while, Grampa taught subtraction in Berlin.
It was easier than inventing electric motors that
might work underwater, but he got slapped, there

was suspicion and distrust, the first inch of his small
intestine went sour, when he looked down thirty
people were sitting on the shoulder of the head

he was unveiling, there was talk of capturing Minsk,
pressing on: Ought to kill you, isn't it true? they said.
Yes, yes, you make me so tired, please the weather

is fine, please I don't mean a word of it, I'm all to
blame, please calm down! The boxcar waited in
the field, cows were there, men came, started

the steam hammers: carbon, oxygen, hydrogen
trading in their long arms until there was balance.
So he pretended to fall, but as far as we know

he's still living, he may get another slap, lose some
fingers, they may remove a gland at the base of his
teeth, but he sleeps, wakes up, eats more straw.

OUT OF HABIT

Standing in the shadow of the table,
scarcely looking at the food I serve
you. What is this stone in the soup?
you ask politely. It's come secretly;
it's not from this region, I whisper.
It feels sorry for itself, it's natural
science out of habit, hinting at
a change in the magnetic field,
small but moving gravely toward
your spoon now, can this stone
mean so little to you? Swallow
it whole! That's it, very good!

WAITING FOR GRAMPA

Your father drives him over for a few pictures
with the family. He's ninety and not against
the move to the nursing home. It's winter,

you're reading the April issue of a magazine,
a story like one of his, of kitchen tables being
pulled apart into beds at night, the whole town

lying there for hours, pillows propped behind
backs, snow falling inch by inch and all they
hoped was large burlap bags filled with straw.

That was Russia, this is Wisconsin. This you must
do when Grampa arrives, Gramma says, Gather
all the drinking glasses in the house together,

paint them all colors, pour sand halfway in,
heavy oil on top, then insert a wick, light it
the moment he comes in. He will bless you

and bless you . . . It was just before the war.
He wrote of not having money to bury a son.
The prelate suggested an egg crate, the body

just fit, so he rented a horse and buggy, tugged
on the reins. All the way to the cemetery, hear him
sing: Oh Life, Life, Without It We Are Dead. Oh . . .

THE STORE

It's a long street with all sorts of stores, one
stands out of the mist. Your father enters it,
the clip black leather bowtie in his pocket,
the cream jacket hangs on a hook. The first
thing he does is dust the perfume counter.
Hours later, before he casts the red sweeping
compound on the floor and looks for the push
broom, in comes your mother for perfume, not
wanting anything else, so he puts the case
back in order. Now comes the sway through
the quiet store. The floorboards are sweet;
he moves over them, whispering, shaking.
At the display window, his hand reaches out
for the switch. Now the lights go out, now they
go on again. They will pulse all night long.

LONG ENOUGH

You tell your father
you're crazy about him.
Every summer, quietly but
so he hears before he dips
both oars in. You run back
for the net you always forget.
You stare at the large fish he
hooks into, are much too young
and full of hope: later you'll

hang your first on the tree,
the headlights cleaning it when
he gets back from town, hugs
you a moment, there's no limit
to the hot light. He's measuring
it now, it's not long enough, it's
never been long enough . . .

THE INTERVIEW

The couple assigned to me has managed
to save a child's violin. They ask me in good
German for a new string. The man starts a story

about planting hawthorns so neighborhood
children would prick themselves if they tried
to climb. Their house in Prague was bombed.

There wasn't an ashtray for the lieutenant.
As a last resort, they tried hiding in a glass
cabinet. I serve them malt-coffee, and we

practice Thank You in English. Finally, the man
finishes the story of their son, who didn't make
it to their eyes when they turned to look.

MY RUSSIAN GRAMMA VISITS ME IN OHIO, EASTER 1963

She comes on a special excuse and must return
immediately or at least in a month. Her baggage
is old Russian newspapers she will wet and wipe
herself with as a precaution against cancer of
the rectum.

She gets off the train by herself but
cannot button her coat. The conductor helps her,
fondles her large ankles, thanks me for the pleasure
since he speaks no Russian. The engineer cools off
in the cornfield, and slowly grows superfluous. It has
been a long ride from Moscow, I imagine.

Gramma
nods, sees the sky yellow, happy there are no hills
or lakes. The snow, she says, must not be interrupted.
On the way to my place, she repairs a button on
my pants, her thread blue with brown stains running
through it.

In spite of the obvious difference between
us, we both yell in Russian at the feed store near town,
greet the bulging eggs, buy two to decorate. Then
she insists we pass the cemetery and the church, likes
the fact they sit on opposite sides of town.

Her voice
does not carry at the cemetery. The house next to mine
she mistakes for a temple, but believes there are no Jews!
On her first trip to America, she wants only one thing: will
the world think I have talent, no or yes? Her gums bleed
so we make a dental appointment. Up in the guest room
I respond more and more to her Russian dialect but draw
back before her elastic bloomers, in which she brings me
the family Bible. It smells sweet as rubber.

I fumble to thank
her the way she would like me to, while she learns to operate
the shower nozzle. Before I can mention the curtain, funny
hairs spatter me. She lobs the pink soap over the rod and I
see her dab some green shampoo on husky nipples. I look
at them closely and think of Russian art. Let me see a towel,
she says, so I hand her one with a map of Moscow I've been
stitching on it, which makes her sad.

I love my sad Russian
Gramma as much as anyone, but Russia needs such sadness,
so at four in the morning I drive her back to the station. She
hardens in the chill but looks alert, climbs into the freight's cab
and begins cleaning it, lifts me up to inspect the job. Then we
take a break among some sleeping cows beside the track.
They are dreaming in Russian and my Gramma lows. We argue
softly all the way back to her childish country, the snow flaking
and falling in a single file into her grave. I hitch my horse
to her headstone, haul it back to Ohio.

A father gives his son supper.
What are you thinking of, boy?
He has a right to know, once
upon a time he will find out what
he wants to know, snatch the boy
up, throw him over his head, go
to the door, climb into the snow
without any hurry. There he is
in his furry cap, shaggy coat,
growing smaller and smaller.

IT'S ZERO

The furnace is out, this time it's
not the pilot light. We're such

damn fools, waiting for a plumber,
letting the cat out, turning the oven

on, building a fire with apple wood,
reciting old Russian poems of cold

in the land, swaying and full of hope
in rocking chairs, the glue holding,

from STORIES MY FATHER CAN TELL

OUT & READY

1

The ice man set a block in the tub,
jammed the pick back in his belt, Ma
turned the sign in the window, 25 cents
next time, Pa went out, got the block,
I put my tongue all over it, got slapped.
From the middle of the street newsboys
shouted, WAR! WAR! Read all about it!

2

Schnooty McKenzie woke me up, Hey,
we're going to make some money, kid,
the war's ending today, come on! So
we ran downtown to the Sentinel, got
a stack of papers. Come on, Eddie-O,
We're not gonna sell 'em in Milwaukee!

3

So we ran all the way to the North Shore
Rapid, jumped out in Kenosha and Racine,
sold them at all the stations. When we got
back late, our pops were standing under
the lamppost, their belts pulled out & ready.

It got so foggy
Mr. Barkin put Bernie
on the front fender, gave
him a flashlight, when they
got to Madison they stopped
in front of a house, Bernie
waited around, walked
in back to see the fence,
it was a nice house, a nice
neighborhood, one hour, two,
Mr. Barkin came out grinning,
started going every week then,
gave Bernie a buck not to tell.

INSIDE

Mr. Ray was a bastard, Heil Hitler from the South,
always standing there, arms crossed, one eye on
his pocket watch, I was the first one in, then Betty,
Nagurski and Bomsleiter the soda fountain manager,
then maybe Flo'd walk in and Clara Zarenner, an old
lady with a nurse's uniform who waited on older ladies
for douche bags, powders, elastic bloomers and Sam
Zuckerman, then Betty Gulke who died of cancer,
they all walked past the cigar counter while Mr. Ray
walked closer to the door. When the girls started up
the big coffee machine and toast, doctors, lawyers
and dentists came in the side entrance, schmoozed
a little, and then exactly at 8 A.M. Mr. Ray locked
the door, proceeded to count everybody inside.

SHOEING HORSES

They did it in front of two huge
water tanks, the moment a horse
came in a man in an apron took off

its hooves with a claw, then he'd
shape each bare hoof with a claw,
hand it to the next man, who painted

in some tar till the crevice filled. A man
in the rear pounded nails in, cut them,
and filed them near the place they
slaughtered the chickens I delivered.

AIRPLANES

We found out there were airplanes,
heard noises, read about them in some
magazines, Schnooty McKenzie came by,

Let's build us one of those airplanes, you guys!
So we went to Shutkin's Drugstore, stole Popular
Mechanics, found a picture of a bright black

airplane. We got to have lath, gobs of cheesecloth
for the wings, Schnooty said, Want a one-seater or two?
The airplane never left the attic till they tore the house

down, because we built her too big. Ma never hung
clothes up there, she always hung them by the furnace.

HAFFA BLOCK

On the way down to the game
one of the Pevners said, Boy, I got
the worst stomach ache, we didn't
pay him any attention, on the way
back home the Pevner kid said,
I can't walk no more, so Bloom
took him haffa block, I took him
haffa block, then Schnooty took him
haffa block till we thought he'd die.

ALL THE BOYS

Knute Rockne had a team, played on
15th & State against Marquette, we got
nuts on football that year, all of us,

the Blooms, Schnooty McKenzie, Stanley,
the other Blooms, and Frankie Chadacek,
who became a pharmacist, the first

vacation he had he took his boys out
to the lake to fish, took a snooze, his boys
went for a swim. When Frankie got up he saw

them floundering, ran like all get out, jumped
in, was able to save one before he drowned.

EVERY YEAR

Every year the fishing gets harder.
You want to doze in your father's arms.
Next best thing you go to the schoolyard,
sit on a swing, watch for falling stars.
A bat swoops low, that's that.

You hire a boat, go down river.
The moon hands over its crown.
All this time not a word.

Fish sitting at one depth
and for half a minute you feel the glory
of not having schemed at all:

the hook you bait takes a little thought.
A man hopes to catch his father a better fish.
Hints of spring in the water, wind pushing
hard to that bare little island every year.
He's fathering there.

ON TEACHING YOUR FATHER TO FLOAT

In the distance, between rows of trees,
a man's stamping his feet in the snow.
He seems to fall, gets up, falls down
again a different way, does this till
I reach him, see for the first time he's
my father, and I look down the way
you would at a giant, slowly bending
your knees, leaning way over, watch it!

Getting him on your back at last, you
spend the night with him up there, trying
to keep your balance. Come morning,
the snow's churned, a sea of fresh water!
You lay him on the surface, his head back,
gently move his arms till he can move them.

AND GIVE LESSONS TO YOUR SON

We start in the shallows, search for
the break, the drop-off. What kind of
bottom is that, Dad? He doesn't seem
to care, he's watching an eagle fish.
It drops as if it's been shot, he says,
pleased with the comparison. I try
to keep him talking, stories of the old
country, standing in cold mountain
streams with his father, moments
spent trying to swim if they heard shots,
and the weeds didn't go over their heads.

Digging and digging, burning, burning
the bottoms of their feet, drying them in
the smoke of a fire if they could. Terrible
murders nearby, just when they sat down
to pray. And I see resemblance: the way
we eat with our hands, order the slave
to destroy the child as soon as it's born.

It'll be a mud bottom, Dad looks down:
Don't do as I did. Fish alone, take your
time. And give better lessons to your son.

Your father's standing at one end
of the room, the light falling into his book.
He makes a mark, one hand acting out
of deep gratitude, the other a stick pointing
in two directions: back to promises, ahead
to thievery. But nothing happens in the first
half hour after he catches you red-handed,
dead to rights. You eat a little, try behaving,
put your arms up.

           The second half hour he asks
good questions: the floor broke the glass? What
curve in what drawer? Little lock in the middle?
With a hairpin? Then a sigh, pushes the money
hard against your hand, runs it through your
fingers, crosses bridges with it, looks dazed all
night long. No argument, just heavy breathing
so the tent falls, don't ask for more, he loves
you less, lays a hand on your shoulder, two
dollars on the floor . . .

THE FALL

Run, Mama! She doesn't or can't,
so I swallow her quickly. She makes

me heavy. I sway to the ground, roll
over. Papa picks me up, puts me in

his cart, agrees she's inside me. I flush
so he looks for water. There is none so

he does the next best thing, sits on me
in the hot sun. Then we shake hands and

have a good talk. Then my easy-going
madman of a father dumps me down

the hill: Mama tears free. It's late when
he finds her. Together they start out to

look for me. I'm a small stone far below.
They scrape me up, skip me across water.

SUBMARINE POEM

1

At first, the interior of the sub seems unbelievably
complicated, a maze of dials, valves, and gauges,
every available inch of space occupied. But listen
to our guide. Though we lose a good deal, and she
talks too much of how cramped the quarters are,
running her hand over the linen-bedecked bunks,
and seems to idolize the enemy captain—carefully
she points to a picture: he's riding a horse on a farm
in Bavaria—she will quit her job just before our tour
is over, press past us: Miss, stop! Stop, Miss! everyone
cries, plunged in grief.

2

                    The movies we see later are
official Navy films taken during the actual battle. We
press both hands to the slatted wooden seats, staring
up at the waves. They go higher and higher, the mind
sliding to the folding top of the washstand which was
the captain's desk when he lowered the lid and drew
the tiny blue curtain.

STRAW

When their wine turned to vinegar, crops
blighted, iron rusted and bees were driven
from their hives, they went mad, begged
for straw from hut to hut, wrapped an old
woman in it and put a match to her. Down
the hill she went, blazing. That's for all your
crimes, they shouted, drinking themselves
drunk. What, what've we done? They poked
each other in the morning. Blamed an old
woman, huh? And so they saw more clearly,
went back to the huts for more straw, this
time they built a straw man, dragged him
through town in a cart so all the people
might see him before they set fire to him
in the fields; a fire so fierce they could make
out a man slipping out of the straw, running.

They were so stunned they threw their hands
to their eyes, turned to face the burning figure:
Old Woman, they cried, We're burning the Old
Woman, they clapped and cried till rain came.

RUN OVER, RUN OVER

In memory of Russell Edson

It's not even your own flesh and blood.
Just a dog you run over on a country road.
You open the door slowly, walk back toward
the spot in the mirror. God, I've killed something,
what the hell was I doing, not watching the road!?

A gate slams. The farmer walking toward you
surprises the hell out of you. Before you can say
a word, he begs your pardon: That damn dog!

If you want to help bury him, mister, there's a spade
over there. I'll get my kids. He picks up the dog by
the hind legs, swings it like a rabbit. Goddamn kids!

You stand there. Maybe you're a little hard of hearing,
suppressing something: we all ought to be related, have
large families to look after. You look over at the spade.
If you picked it up, you'd throw it clear out into the field.

THE APRON

The man's been pitying himself all Sunday long.
First he went down cellar to oil the generator, see
what the potatoes were doing. Then he took a few
baits from his tackle box, paint wearing, hooks
falling off. When he put the last fish of the season
back into the water it sank down to the bottom,
left a long streak of blood trailing like a ribbon.

He dragged the boat to the car. In the mirror
the lake was greasy and thick. He put his foot
on the gas. It was like stepping on the woman's
apron; a pleasant apron with bees and flowers
all over. The kettle was singing. And steaming.

When the man gets home there's nothing at
the end of a stringer in his hand. When the child
runs between the man and the woman she
makes strange sounds they can't understand.
When they put her to sleep in a glass bed at
night, they look in from all sides till it dawns.

AND ANOTHER

Before I sharpen the knife I look over
at the other eye, which tilts if the tail
slaps the plate; tilts or rises, would rise
all night in the empty kitchen, throw
away memory. I press it back down
with a thumb, it's the end of the 20th
century; fish in Loon Lake are scarce.

I should scale them before leaving for
home, the old fisherman says, watching
his bobber drift into weeds. "So the slime
don't freeze," he puffs. But the markings
go, I want to say, don't you know that?!

Oops, think I just touched a tongue, right
there! Soft gray petal, must be its tongue.
Hey, kids, come here, show you something.
When they come running to the sink, I put
a hand up: We won't be eating this fish
tonight, it's not enough, need to get more.
(Dad, that's what you always say . . .).
That's enough now or I'll lose my temper!

They're frightened, I know, keep adding up
the ones I've caught since buying the boat.
Still, on such a day, there the fish was, all by
itself, down by that stump. Then it splashed;
all I did was pick up anchor, row over, give
it my smallest minnie. When I cut in, the kids
giggle, the fish seems to fart a little. So I wash
it off, hurry it into a plastic bag and, having
sentenced it to freezing, blow on my hands,
hug the kids—the only thing that could still
their hunger is another fish, and another.

60

WHISPERING TO THE GUARD

I open my eyes.
The painting I want
is in the smallest room
of the museum. There's
an old man gazing at it,
whispering to the guard.

Between two blue ash,
snow growing darker and
the little bed in the corner
burning till morning.

from THE DARMSTADT ORCHIDS

TEACHING MY GRAMPA
TO READ ENGLISH

When we begin, he hits the table with his fist,
picks his teeth, Oh, I could eat these tiny words,
he cries in Russian. Crowded on the table, ink,
a pen, and heavenly white paper that reminds
him of snow in the old country. No bat I know can
resist the dawn, he says, lays his head down on
the desk a while till a lightning bolt jolts him awake:
Ready for more now! You be a good boy, teach
me all you know, he says, sets his pocket watch
straight by the kitchen clock. Ready, all you know
in twenty minutes, then I'll have to start the chores.

I want to breathe in a cloth and lay it on his lips.
I want to go to the window with him to watch it
start to rain without a dumb word between us.
I want to help him muck the barn, I want I want
I want. When he heads down cellar, I daydream
till he comes up with a hammer he holds out:

Now, again, he says, It must be like driving in
the rusty spike on which we'll come to hang.

THE HUNGARIAN TELEPHONOGRAPH

It was the first of its kind anywhere, and no one
seemed to know who invented it. Great grampa
signed up for one. The day it arrived, the whole
neighborhood appeared to see it installed above
the couch. "For reclining listening," the ad said.

You didn't talk into it. What was the point of that?
Great gramma said. All you did was lie back and
listen to things coming across the precious wire
from the central station: days there'd be news,
stock reports, lectures the government selected.
Great-grampa was glad of that. He couldn't read
and arranged to stay home from the factory so
he could learn everything. Nights, workers hauled
the sender to the opera at The People's Theater.

Once, when they tuned it to the big earthquake
out east, people tapped on each other's doors:
Praised Be Thy Most Holy Sacrament! They yelled
back and forth across the square. The inventor,
terrified, almost chopped his leg off at the asylum.

EVERY PART OF THE PIG
BUT THE SQUEAL

Changing live hogs into chops, other cuts,
requires a killing floor, a shackling pen, drains,
a motorized hoist, sticking and bleeding rails,
salting vats, de-hairing machinery, a moving
chain to carry the hogs along, now let's go
see the sprays for washing, burners to singe
the fine hairs, weighing and inspecting tables
where you'll be stationed, my step-grampa
said, who'd just married Gramma and one
benefit was, the family said, I could have
a job that stifling summer.
                    I'd watch them
park and kiss out the bay-window when he'd
bring her back from Steuben Hall for lectures
on the New Russia. I didn't know much then,
but the McCarthy hearings were starting and
I knew from kitchen whispers that Gramma was
frightened. Later, everyone blamed her cancer
on Joe the Ogre. Thinking back now I'm glad
I couldn't stick the job out. But when Gramma
got much worse, I got sick a lot. The doc said
it was hyperventilation, gave me a paper sack
to breathe into and the rest of the summer we
set a place for Gramma at cards, even though
she couldn't leave her bed.
                         I'd run to tell her
who won after every hand, show my losing cards.
Never mind winning and losing, she said, How
come you resent my marriage to Isidore? You
grew up on his meat, look at you! So, he was
a bit crude, believed things you couldn't accept,

so what? She was arched against the headboard,
and pa said later she probably died the moment
I passed my exams. I drove Grampa's old meat
truck back from Madison so fast I spun on all
the tears that had turned to ice.

BIBLICAL STUFF

Way back when they built pens around the sassafras trees,
berries fattened the pigs, gave them a clean, healthy look.

Something you wouldn't mind eating if you had to, children
yelling and hollering till fathers came home, made sure doors

were locked. Mine was The Sauerkraut Man, they told me.
He'd cut cabbage into tiny bits, throw the best into a barrel,

the rest to the pigs. Mother, they said, was The German Cook,
working away in Paris, introducing sauerkraut and smoked herring.

They said she taught the goofy young king to eat those things,
but no one believed her. Gramma twisted her hand round and

round, singing, *Kosinka, kosink-a, ko-sink-a!* Father took mother's
face in his hands. Now, that's a face, he'd sing, whirling her round

and round. Here a face, there a face, everywhere a face face,
they'd dance till they fell down. Then he stuck his head between

her legs. Looks like something alive in there, he said. And I was
born, just like that. And the whole crowd laughed to see such

sport, until it dawned on them something had truly been born.

HARVEY TELLS US ABOUT
FROMAN THE BUTCHER

for & with H.G.

You know he's a concentration camp survivor,
don't you? Had that shop in Cleveland that was
robbed. Well, he was shot up pretty good, but now
he's in Lorain. We just love him, and he even sings
the cantor stuff beautifully, but I like it best when
I walk into his market:

Hello, Mr. Froman. I'm Harvey Gittler.
I know.
My wife died a year ago.
I know that too, I'm sorry.
And I've recently remarried.
That I also know.
My new wife doesn't know too much about Passover.
I know, so what else is new?
She sent me for some horseradish.
I know, he says, reaches down below
the counter, hands over a whole one!
Mr. Froman, I only need a little piece.
Take it, take the whole thing,
a wedding present from Froman the Butcher!

SOMEWHERE IN EAST GERMANY

We got ready to catch the train, ran
into its arms, you might say. That's
how happy we were to leave . . .

In good health too, we were, so we drank
plenty of apricot brandy in the dining car
once we got rolling when suddenly men

in guns and boots stopped us, their dogs
sniffing the undercarriages. But we're not
there yet, someone said, What does this

mean? We all nodded, repeating her words
before they motioned us out beside the train
so we could hear the loudspeaker better:

Now return to the train for your belongings,
the voice thickened, so we rushed back. We'd
left everything behind on board. Carrying our

ashy suitcases down the road to some barracks,
we thought they might at least serve us some of
Gramma's strudel—a lame joke, because all

sorts of other matters came up, for which no one
was prepared. We started sweating, tiptoed to
a tiny window, saw the train starting to puff, as

if its journey were making a deep impression on
the engineer. Back in line, we began memorizing
world capitals, thinking we had plenty of time left.

Gramma was walking slowly toward us now, her
head shaking: What I'm going to tell you is awful,
awful, I said awful, was all we remember she said.

THE TIME WE THOUGHT
WE COULD STEAL

On our lunch break we spread out in a chain from
the Chesterfield cigarette display to the door of
Ackerman's Drugstore, pretending to be interested
in nose drops, hydrogen peroxide, Ex-Lax, whatever
happened to be on the shelf near us, and when old
Ackerman turned his back I'd knock a pack loose,
slide it along with my foot to the next kid and so on
down the line. We'd wait till a fresh customer came
in and use the space behind him to kick the smokes
into the street. For weeks, two or three packs we got
every time we shared after school when somehow
Ackerman got wise. Using one of those new mirrors
we didn't know existed, he caught us cold, lined
us up behind the prescription counter, proceeded
to call our fathers one by one. When he got to mine,
I overheard my pop yelling, You can forgive a young
man for going wrong with girls, but for God's sake don't
go easy on my kid now! All the while, Ackerman took
notes, shoved the phone away, climbed up on his high
stool, adjusting his glasses before he said solemnly:
Gentlemen, among officials we have lots who steal
and we don't know it. On all sides vanity and greed
puff up. Some of the worst of us pretend to drink like
prophets from the river, but do you know how many
we shall catch stealing with mirrors? Well, speak up,
I can't hear you! He answered himself, because who
could talk? To begin with, a man gradually gets used
to stealing, especially if he doesn't have a job, he said
in a hush. With that he clipped little black bowties to
our collars and marched us down to the basement
to start sweeping till the dirt disappeared. Exhausted,

hours later, fallen asleep in the aisles among the stock,
our fathers found us with our heads on Mrs. Ackerman's
pillows, awakened by their hard steps coming down.

THE DIARIES

Entries pointing to her last moon.
Virginia's trying not to look at the water.

The right place to look at it. Out over it.

Touch it the way a fish tries touching
the stippled sand. She's close to shore.

Under the lilies, the rose bobbing, the pad
moving back to where it was and her feet

shoeless.

And high over the Channel
the German planes

and the fish in the moon

cold.

IT'S GOOD FOR POETS TO LIVE ON IN PROSE

with thanks to Ilse Aichinger
& In memory of Günter Eich & Miroslav Holub

A great poet was dying. There was nothing modern medicine
could do. Just before saying goodbye, the poet's wife held
the doctor back a moment. "I don't want to wake up one
morning with Günter dead beside me," she said. "Isn't there
some sign I might have the end is coming?" The doctor lit up.
"As a matter of fact I'm interested in the very phenomenon.
I've found if you give the patient simple little problems, nothing
too complex mind you, he should be able to do them quickly
if he's all right. Something like 2x2, or 3x3, nothing much harder.
Twice a day; once when he wakes up mornings, and again
before he turns in for the night. If he has any trouble, the end
is near. That sounds crazy, my dear, but I've found it to be so."

So she proceeded to give him a little dose of arithmetic that
very night. For a while all went well. Then one day, picking
apples in the orchard, just beyond the veranda where he lay
watching, she set about counting. "Exactly 100 apples, I've
picked exactly 100 apples!" she said aloud and hurried to
his side. "I was just picking apples, you were watching me,
remember?" she said. "Well, I got to 99 when I saw one more
out the corner of my eye. Now, Günter, how many does that
make, 99 plus 1?" He raised himself up holding to her arm.

"Wait, wait a minute, I know the answer, oh such an easy one!"
he said but sank back down, his face drawing sweat. Feverish,
he lay there searching for the answer. Time stopped. She began
to tremble. She was ready for this moment in her mind, but not
in her body. Finally, as if by some miracle, his eyes cleared and
he relaxed. "I've got it," he murmured. "It's 100, think of that!"

She hugged him, wiped his face and gave him a little water from the glass by his cot. Then she started to leave, but like

a bad actress who turns around in the door for one more word, she said, "Günter, those 100 apples, remember? Well, what if we took one away, what then? 100 minus 1, how many now, Love?" Again, the little scene played itself out for an eternity.

He fell back on the pillow and she shuddered. "Easy, such an easy one," he said from time to time, tapping her on the arm. It seemed as if an hour had passed this time, when his eyes cleared. "I don't know that anymore," he whispered. And died.

First King was assassinated, but the skies overhead
remained clear, the swans on the lake regularly fed,
but when Kennedy's followed, whole trams of Swiss
burst out crying. They rushed back to their flat, tried
tuning the rented radio to a station they could hear.

Paris, it's Paris, she screamed, while he wired antennas
to kitchen pipes for more sound: two journalists and an
old philosopher putting it all in perspective. Then choirs

and violins and the sound going dim. They slapped
the pipes, the sun making little spots on the tiles by
their feet. They hugged and cried, hugged and cried.

MEXICAN POSTCARDS

for Jane / Mom & in memory of Günter Eich

1

Dogs and children. Waiting for garbage.
Farther out, sharks on the second wave
just before it breaks.

2

The man sells you a belt.
It's a good price for you,
a good price for me, Senor.

3

Cortez crumpled a piece of paper.
The mountains of Mexico! he cried,
and threw it on the dirty table.

4

Rags hanging across the road.
Welcome signs of poor villages.

5

Farther up the hill, a thick shock of broom.
Three girls all in white emerging from a tin hut.
A cemetery & Mary Carmen's Eatery all webbed up.

6

An old woman in black, leaning on a gold cane,
whispering a dirty joke to the bartender. He likes it;
she gets a tequila, drinks it straight down, judging.

7

The people on the next balcony look over.
The moment you look back, they turn on a fan.

8

Today, no boats risk going to the islands.
You lift the mattress, plunge a hand into
all the money you have.

9

The little girl dancing with the rooster on her arm!

10

And the women washing clothes, drawing them
over huge rocks. You used to throw your handkerchief
up with a stone. It came down covered with cloth.

THE DARMSTADT ORCHIDS

Horst ran a tank halfway
into Russia, then they blew
his leg off. Now he raises
the most delicate orchids
behind his cottage near
Darmstadt, Merck City, House
of Chemicals for whoring
and healing. No wonder
the Brits bombed it to bits.

We argue the necessity of it
till we almost come to blows,
when Horst says, It's the one town
where Goethe could be himself.
Bauhaus came later, and Auden
was assigned to intelligence duty
right after the war there, days
interrogating former Nazis, nights
liberating wine, drinking it to bits,
sleeping it off in a Jeep.

In the morning, Horst takes me
to the station. I hear you have
a hard time too, he says, With
your life, your country's. We start
brooding, a decent German,
an American Jew, not angry,
not quarreling anymore.

THE BEAR HE SEES

I don't see it but I hear it. Lapping
a drink the way we guzzle beer after
a hot game. Then silence again . . .

Pinching a brown fly from my tackle,
I work the other side of the boat now.
There it is again, Dad, my son says.

The shore stares back, hesitation's
in the air. Surely there's time for more
life, seeing a bear, feeling more animal,

thinking lost thoughts, drying some fears.
Don't worry about the bear, son. It's spent
a long time as a cub, learning its place

in the world. But he's not worried at all,
just goes on seeing, There, over there now!
Dad, don't you see him at all? I admit I

don't. Talk to them sometimes but never
seem to see one, so I work from memory.
Bears get bad-mannered only if we enter

their realm, I whisper. The bear's in the lake
now, and of course I see him at last, shaping
a fish, launching his hunger. Skilled apparition!

STEP BY STEP

I get up, make breakfast, see the children off,
go to work in an office, come home for lunch,
at which point my head aches. I try identifying
exactly what I think I'm doing, wrong that is.

Everyone thinks well of me, I suppose. But one day
it happens: marching to the far end of the den, I
look back through the dining room to the sink in
the kitchen. So, I think, that's the route, the way
you'll always walk in hunger; and I open a window,
slip slowly through. Now that I'm going step by step
evening comes on nice and slow by the time I'm in
the middle of the street, taking a little breath, closing
an eye. The best light's gone. I remember I wanted
to force some things, I remember the cat's limp but
little of the dog. I remember if you want to catch big
fish, keep to half-clear water, the middle. If you look
to shore, there's a steepled house with an old man
tucked in bed reading all this while. Call him Doppel-
gänger but keep on going. Even if it's really late, he
lights his dock, just keep on rowing, all the way to sea.

Push it farther out,
like a model ship. Wind
comes up, blows it along.
Next a wave, casts it along.

Back on shore, watching,
hands trembling, whisper,
There, I did that for you.

Love's on its own now, doesn't
make a sound. Just look on
with a few words on your lips.

Time to spread your hands out,
a cover for what's left. Let wind
wind blow harder, waves swell.

FUNERAL PIE

Usually raisin, with a latticed top,
served right after we finish the last
of the cold ham and chicken. Later,
on the way back home, we stop for
for another slice at the Dutch eatery
off the pike, where it's always on
the menu; and if you have another
piece, it's as though you can speak
a foreign language, say things which
can be made to go with food after
someone dies; someone not your
mother: you look at her through
the smoke, blow her a kiss
If you're lucky, there will be one or
two more years left to move closer
before it's her turn. Unless, as she
says, You die first, something
a parent most fears.

For a child to die, she looks hard
into my eyes, Is to drown everything
else, mix violence with love in a way
no human can fathom—and then
she swipes a piece of my pie after
getting me to fall for some bird out
the window, which is never there.

NEXT CAT

Here are some things my daughter and I
went over when she entered the clinic
for treatments and I said we'd be glad
to house-sit her cat, Friskies, warts and all:

Do you know how to apply CPR?
(To a drowning cat?)

How you get her to drop a bird?
(Throw a stone past her ear?)

Read to her!
(Pour her some brandy, too?)

And please don't pull her up by her ears!
(The way President Johnson used to treat
his hounds? Always thought they loved it.)

And talk to her a lot, Dad.
(I'll keep her up nights, don't worry.)

After the first treatment, she's silent a moment.
And here I am, perfectly calm. I said I was calm.

ON WIGS

We're watching Sophocles in Athens.
It's her first evening out since deciding
on a wig to hide effects of radiation.

The Greeks got it right. Black for tyrants,
blond for heroes, red for comic servants.
The early Church did its part: frowned

on wigs as evil. Along came Louis XIII,
prematurely bald, so back they came.
From *perruque* to *periwig* to *wig,* we

shorten as we lengthen. In an old book,
I see the 18th Century produced more
than 40 types: pigeon's wig, comet,

spinach seed, artichoke, boar's head,
moving freely among flora and fauna.
Some women owned them all in tints.

Shaving off our own hair, donning others'
is right up there with Pepys, whom we've
taken to reading at this time in our lives.

He wore his own hair for a wig! But I still
can't fathom this: when we confess sins,
you in yours God must know are more

guiltless than the rest of us. I turn back
the covers, take you in my arms. Wait,
you whisper, Nobody kisses me in mine;

and you toss it clear across the room.
When you wag your head, the whole
world's a stage again, curtain going up!

MARBLES IN MILWAUKEE

for AC

After shooting marbles all afternoon in the alley,
I dumped a pocketful of white bibbies, striped
plasters and bullies on my desk. My shooter,
a blood-alley, streaked with red, always came
out last. I put them back in their stable, an old
Chinese Checkers box under the bed, the shooter
facing all the others from its own corner. When
arcing away from between my cocked thumb
and crooked forefinger, it knocked its share of
plebes out of the circle. But it preferred solitude
to the most brilliant games; dressed in its creamy
reds it looked more like a tiny Mars than any real
sight on Earth. When Borges asked me fifty years
later what I remember most liking as a child: *Exactly,*
he whispered, Tell me *exactly,* I froze at first. Finally,
he poked me with his cane till I blurted out: Wiping
my shooter coated with dust as clean as I could, Sir.
He tipped his head back, and there was that same
red at the bottom of his eyes sliding into view.

THE EMPTY SCHOOLROOM

A few sparrows assemble in the rafters.
A stripe detaches from the flag's shadow,

moves into isolation on the dusty blackboard.
Lincoln's left eye seems to stray. The books on

the desks say aloud: Then we shall serve the Lord
our God! What a terrible line of poetry, the Frost

Reader replies, and the custodian comes along,
plinks chopsticks on the piano, closes it again.

And no one squeals or shouts, laughs or claps
hands as if carried away. And no one asks,

How much did the grocer give Mrs. Clark back
if she gave him $10 for 3 cans of soup; 33¢ each?

The front door's open, but no one's there to survey
the wide space that becomes the road, as we've

done who pledged Allegiance and were carried so
far away, passengers forgiven our simple answers.

NEVER

Chinese pheasants used to be
all around the farms out here.

Brought from China, we suppose.
Some 16-18 inches high, 2 lbs. or so,

red cone, red breast, heavy neck
feathers, honk like geese and we

used to eat them now and then
till they turned up in Ming Lan's story.

Sent from China, she's in town now
on a hunt for a new life—her parents

having coughed up over $10,000 to
spring her, we hear. She's not told us

the worst. We head out to Miller's for
home-made ice-cream, sit at a picnic

table behind the store, while we lick
watching the field beyond for signs

of life. When we spot the bird, tell Ming
it's hers, she shakes her head, watches

it peck along. You're the ones who
eat it, she says quietly. We never did.

PICASSO'S WOMAN WITH
ONE BREAST EXPOSED

I was so afraid of her up there over my crib,
I couldn't sleep. My parents meant no harm
hanging her over me, a sort of aging Penthesilea,
looking over the infant Achilles, I heard my father
say and my mother took his hand for withdrawing.
Bunging my mouth with a bit of thumb, I turned
away to live. She'd bend down, her downcast
eye smiling, waiting for me to grow up worthy.

Now, well past the middle of life, I've known women
who've lost theirs to cancer, toast them with a midnight
glass of water by my bedside: Aunt Jessie, Gramma Bess
from Chicago, Al Jordan's mother, Miss Joseph my dear
trig teacher, my father's drugstore clerk, and sweet,
sweet Lila, a friend's wife, who's taught us to carry on.

Some nights, I get up to walk a little in the direction
they've gone. If that seems helpless, it is. Oh, I know
it is and when I get sick, I write nothing but nonsense
to another woman I barely know, who's had hers
removed. Lately, I figure if I keep after my wife and
daughter to check theirs, that's doing *something*;
but of course I can't imagine being interfered with
like that. Something never dreamt of, which festers.

DAMFOOLSKIS

Sometimes we wished Uncle Abe'd been just
Mr. Buttinski, or even Allrightski, the thing of it was
he didn't stop there. When the cards were dealt,

the pennies stacked, the vane of inclination swung
in the direction of family forgiveness, Abe upped and
started in on Dad. That bad deal left us at the mercy

of our wants, but Dad never meant any harm, even
let me break my piggybank to invest. We'd drive round
and round the land the family compound was to be

built on, later the samovar would be dusted off. Hurry
Gramma said, I can't last much longer. Abe fell through
the cracked window into the cellar, months of collars

around his burly neck followed, not to mention a scary
leg brace he'd snap off, chase me with till Mom gave
him what for. Lately, Abe's stopped living altogether,

the family's been busted up, a couple of us aren't even
in the States much, but Abe keeps the stupid cards coming:
If it weren't for your Pop, we'd be all together and cozy.

Hell, I keep writing back fast, Dad couldn't know it was
a scam, no one saw dark signs, we all drew curtains so
the sunlight fell from our dumb faces; and besides, Dad's

paid enough by now, Abe, compared with which your
troubles are a bunch of grapes. P.S. At the sanitarium, Dad
hears the Lord say, Go, befriend other families until one

appreciates
YOU
at last.

UNDERSTANDING POETRY

for Ilse Aichinger & Günter Eich

The last time I saw him, the summer we visited at his villa near Salzburg, one of us screwed up her courage to ask for his autograph. He'd just come up from the cellar, insisting on bringing up another case of Coke, quick to point out he could still get it in the old green bottles. "Only if you have a ball-point pen, Fräulein Sally, I love how they work," he said, wiping the sweat from his face with the checkered cowboy handkerchief I'd given him on my last visit.

Pen in hand, he beckoned us to follow out to the veranda. We went along, school children on a walk to the museum. From a bell jar on the sideboard, he carefully rolled away one long, thin cigarette from the arched pile—Turkish, I realized, from his early poems—the way one plays Pick-Up-Sticks. We formed a half-circle around him, Sally stepping slightly forward. He licked his lips, wet the pen, then wrote his name with a tiny flourish next to the Turkish script on the cigarette. "There," he said, handing it to Sally, "Now let's relax in the garden and listen to your air force on its way over our Alps."

We coaxed him into reading one more poem with the last of his voice that day—he'd had surgery on his vocal chords, but the radiation had gone well, he assured us. "Besides, my doctor likes me to read aloud a little, stretches things down there." When a jet slashed past, he paused mid-sentence. "There, that's enough, your people want the last word, see you next year perhaps—did you like the sandwiches? I may have some dark beer next time for those of you old enough to drink it legally," he grinned.

Christmas, the first of his cards came. *"Mein Lieber,* has Sally smoked it up yet?" I had to think a while: Lordie, typical of you, Günter! Sally was still at school, so I called on the pretext of wanting to show her a certain book. I knew he wouldn't want me to ask her directly, so I sort of wondered aloud, What ever happened to that autographed cigarette? I was hoping you'd ask, she said, There it is on the mantle. And there it was all right, under a little glass bell, fairly aglow, the signature alive, looking a little Turkish!

And so our correspondence started up in earnest. I wrote back, Dear G, nope—on the oldest postcard I could find, for his beloved collection—Not yet. And every three or four months, for the next year or so, he'd write, sometimes just, Yet? Once, his card said,Is it thin air, finally? I'd try to find out, write back, and on and on until Sally graduated, moved away. Dear G, I recall writing then, I'll have to save some money to check on the cigarette again. Sally's gone to China. . . .

Ilse, Günter's great love, handed me the last card in our exchange, which never got sent. I'd come to visit, but he'd died a week before. I stared down hard at the tiny script: *Lieber,* I guess she never really understood my poems at all.

"LIKE BEAMS THAT MAKE A TENT OVER THE CHURCH AT NIGHT"

—Virginia Woolf

But they were searchlights, and it was war.
When we think of agonies like hers, no one

should have done all she did. Leonard would
forget the lemon, she to cook the haddock after

one of those days, conceding almost everything,
conceding nothing. In my dream she's a peasant

in a shabby coat, throwing crusts to some swans
along the bank, refusing to fall in with the plan to

drown this time. It would be so good, I think, if
she were still alive, agreed to speak to us, with

our pathological thirst for the right word, and I
imagine no one dared to finish her sentences.

Reading back to front, I come across this entry,
Wednesday, 6 September 1939: "No raids yet.

Poland being conquered & then—we shall be
attended to." I suspect our predisposition for

insanity is for our own amusement. . . . Earlier,
1936 now, Kipling's dead and the king's dying.

How *is* the Empire? he is said to have said with
his final breath. And was told it was doing fine.

FRIED SHIRT

You've got your fried shirt on, Gramma would say.
We loved the way she said it, fingered the pearly
buttons before she'd put hands to hips, step back
for one more look, "Just to visit me!" She shook
her head, grinned that Old World way, lopsided.
She'd entered life with very little hope, in Senice,
which till a while ago brimmed with Russian tanks,
though the church on the square's still the same.

I don't know what I would or could have said to her,
if she were alive to hear of my visit right before the dam
broke, and Russia wasn't Russia anymore. Perhaps that,
roaming the cobblestones, the people still seemed
as friendly as she would often recall, even in their
wretched little houses. Wind-puffs dust your shirt.

She went to the seamstress school for girls in town,
one building I asked permission to visit. They gave her
an iron when she graduated she used till her dying day,
a universe away. The school's still there, but there's
barbed wire fencing around it now, which won't
come down for a while, and some sort of guard
at the gate, who couldn't understand what little
Czech I know. I toyed with the idea of showing him
her picture, leaning over the hot iron, perplexed,

We'll never have a quiet world again, she'd say,
Never ever in a hundred thousand million years.

CHILDREN AND ROCKING CHAIRS

Have you not noticed, it's the first
piece of furniture children will go to,
even in a crowded room? They stand
there a while, pondering aloud how
it works, in that double-echo voice,
feet fixed as iron. They they'll smile,
extend a finger, put some muscle
into the notion. The chair moves!
Next, half a hand goes to work.

Occasionally, you see them sitting
in the rocker in the corner, quiet but
a frown to their brow, letting a small
doll fall from their lap, gazing toward
the sky with closed eyes, arms crossed,
the world below made one and if you
dab at their eyes, they will cry out, but
next thing you know they're running
about again, greedy for more life,
their restlessness returned. You wish
them all the joy they can ferret out,
see J.F.K. resting his bad back in that
white highchair someone fastened
rockers to so it could creak and creak.

HAIRY WOODPECKER

Not a single hair on its body so how
did it get its name? Should have to
do with *haunting,* which is what it
does to our orchard all spring long.

If apple trees had oil, we'd be rich from
all the wells it's sunk into them, its body
swollen with insects like a drowned man,
but then it hop-steps so fast to new holes

it can barely keep its feet. The very spot
it now stands I call Little Vilna, in memory
of Gramma, who planted such a tree and
loved such a bird before the Nazis came.

EGG ROAST

In memory of Marin Sorescu

It's Easter in Romania again,
more exactly, in the plain of
the Black Sea, where eggs are
cooked with mud, roasted in
a fire no one sits around to sing
any sort of song, because at
this moment, people are about
to step off the ferry, confused
and lonely in their own land,
and the dreadful swelling on
their heads just won't go down.

VISITING ROBERT FRANCIS WITH MY SON

We ask about the crayoned poems;
there's a heap of them, you can't take
your eyes away. Oh, he says, I try to write
one every day now. I surely like Crayolas,
doesn't everyone? Reaching over, he
knocks the orange to the floor. Please
don't bother, I need to fetch it, he says,
lowers his arthritic shape down notch by
notch to the knee by hanging on tight
with both hands to desk. We look away
while he takes many more moments
getting back up—There she is, he grins,
Now I can do another one in orange!
We wave off an offer to make tea.

It's the usual sweet time everyone reports
having in his cheerful company, from a walk
about the yard to the request for a photo—
he's standing between two hubcaps he
"liberated" from an abandoned Jeep,
planted in the grass by the door. We're
worried we're tiring him, but he says, Have
any questions before you go? Well, my son
wonders, taking in all the wood to the cabin,
thinking fire of course, Do you keep all your
poems here, sir? Oh no, my boy, Francis winks,
They're in a nice safety box in the town bank!

from NEAR OCCASIONS OF SIN

I'VE RAISED MY HAND AGAINST

Some who've mentioned my shortcomings
in public, some who've looked me in the eye,
some who've drunk more than I, some much
less, some who were idols, some who didn't know
some things that are wrong are sometimes right,
some who might have said something different
if I'd listened, some who could see through my
deceptions, and some who couldn't, some I
just plain felt sorry for, some who kept me from
even more trouble, some who were too pleased
to see me, some who called me flat-nose kike,
some who cried uncle too soon, some who
wanted me out of the way, some who saw
my face bending over them and told me to
get lost, and once a bat that came out of
nowhere, a horse I couldn't whip, the devil
in the details, and most terrible of all, when
you slowly sat down, put your elbows on
your knees and covered your lovely face
with your hands . . .

DO YOU LOVE ME

When other birds leave off following a ship,
the albatross is left, continues to circle, again
and again, alighting on a wave, dropping
back a while till it reappears, just like that!

Coleridge thought it flew without lifting a wing,
but he never saw one, that pink face convulsing
when it minded what it saw. Rilke drew flamingos
at the Paris zoo, but it's clear from the poems

he dreamt of albatross, while In Zurich the Joyces
circled the aviary till they realized there were none
at all. Greenstreet preferred them to falcons, and
Bogart once gave Lupino a pet one she eventually

had stuffed. Monroe had its concrete likeness made
for her tub. Do you love me, she'd say in that sexy,
ingratiating way, while Porter worked and worked
to get one aboard Ship of Fools, who knows where.

Rothko tried sketching one from a book when he
was six, but O'Keeffe thought it too holy to frame.
When I meet mine, I think it'll be Sunday night, we'll
knit brows together till one of us yanks his head away.

It's no use trying to make it feel to home, Gramma says,
while Grampa snarls from his rocker, In Budapest we used
to say, It's reason enough to hurry faster out of this sad life.

BANDUDELUMS

What we used to call running across
thin shore ice quaking under our feet.

If you were lucky, it bent but didn't break.
Even Gramma finally conceded falling in

and drowning might not be such a bad
death—the cold would surely stun your

fear; she of the worst case scenarios would
push her glasses up, pinch those pale eyes

and say, What more can I say? Some years
later, seeing her through stomach problems,
complications set in. Briefly she broke through

the spiking fever: Let's go bandudeluming,
she whispered. We looked at one another

the way you do to fake understanding, our
long-term memory not up to hers. Sure, Oma,

sure thing, but you've got to cooperate, beat
this thing, then we will . . . Will what, she cried,

more lost than ever. Will what . . .? Desperation
piling up like shore ice, Grampa said, Will make

it home by dark, my darling, and not get spanked.

A FOOT OFF THE BOTTOM

That's simple, Horst said, Snip the end off
a No. 9 hook so it's nice and blunt, attach
the tiniest segment of a worm, then jig
your line down a foot off the bottom.
We were after spiny dogfish, as voracious
a shark as any, in a cove on the North Sea,
under a gray and white sky, fall falling fast.
Horst unwrapped our sandwiches, I pulled
up the beers cooling in the tide. Perfect.

There's little demand for the spiny's flesh
in the States, but in Germany it's highly
prized; not used as meal for farm animals,
Horst said, who's a good man, forced to
fight at fifteen and lost a leg at Stalingrad,
which we don't talk about much anymore.
The silence piled up around us, and my mind
drifted down to where there used to be U-boats—
an image shot up from somewhere: slipper linings
for crews were woven from hair of Jewish women,
one of those facts you can't digest, a bezoar
of sorts, souring your stomach, worse than seeing
that single baby shoe under glass at Yad Vashem.
Horst had wept till I pulled him away to the next
exhibit. Exactly why would you learn to pass as
a native, especially since your Oma said it's
the language of the enemy? Horst had flown
over to pay his respects when she died.

I don't understand it myself, and when Horst
started pushing for reasons again on that dreary,
do-nothing day, I suddenly ripped my clothes off,
dove down far as I could without bursting a lung.

Through the mottled yellows and browns, I made
out a large school of spinys, swimming slowly under
our lures, not interested at all, those tell-tale spots on
their sides, portholes through which nothing escapes.

JABALINA

A small, wild hog with great big teeth, up
around fifty pounds, hard flesh that can come
charging at you if you're careless. I made it
to the tree in time, while my Swabian uncle
shot it dead at my feet. He'd just been given
permission to hunt again by the authorities in
The French Zone, who returned his rifle when
they learned he'd hidden a Jewish wife with
farmer friends in their barn loft those fateful
years. It's yours, he said to the lieutenant, I
shot it for your men. If you use my wife's recipe
you'll never have a better feast, but please
use the Spanish name—*Wildschwein* is what
we called the Nazis. The lieutenant saluted,
and I made my way down the tree for a photo
with the carcass, pulled its bloody head back
until the enormous yellow fangs showed.

YAD VASHEM

I keep to the place in line till it's time
to enter the exhibit, but one look at

the first plaque and I'm back at the end
again, bolting before the guard can check

my stub. Been trying for days now to get
past the field of tiny flames flickering across

the cast-bronze map of all the death camps,
whose names you know by now. It's a tiny

room, and everyone takes tiny steps, so I've
got time to circle around while they head for

the next exhibit. It's hard walking with shackles
on your legs, a young boy says when I stare at

him too long. Then he jumps up and down, makes
a ton of goofy faces and wiggles his ears till we all

get so tired of laughing we could sleep away the rest
of whatever's left of our lives, the air piling up so deep

around us you only see eyes as far as the eye can see.

ASLEEP IN OHIO

Shhh, my wife says, I hear some noises
downstairs. Wake up quietly, I'm scared.

We don't own a gun, so I grab a net
in the corner I use on inside summer

bats that are a major source of rustling
whooshes above our sleeping heads in

this old house, and barefoot my way
down the back stairs to the kitchen.

The moon's half lit, some stars are out,
and when I lower my gaze there he is,

hair mussed, suit torn, face ablaze in
agony, pushing against the screen,

mumbling something I can't understand.
He looks so scared himself I throw open

the door: God God, man, what's with you?
He stumbles toward a chair, blurting out,

Can't sleep a wink in my tower anymore,
can't focus, starting to make bad decisions,

need some heavy-duty R&R, so I thought I'd
parachute down on a small town in Ohio and,

well, here I am. Hope to hell you'll be able to
put me up a bit, could care less if the sheets

haven't been washed lately. My wife's at
my side now, motioning like crazy, so I excuse

myself for a moment. In the hall, she almost
shouts, It's Donald Trump! I just saw his press

conference on the tube this morning! What'll
we do? Come on, think! Well, for starters let's

just get him up to bed, so we each take him
by an elbow and ease him up till his head

flops on my shoulder. He's starting to REM now,
his blotchy eyelids flutter. We push and pull him

up the spiral staircase, make it to a bed, and
down he goes like a sack of potatoes. My wife

takes his shoes off, I loosen his tie. She covers
him with an old afghan, lightly removes his

toupee, so matted I make a mental note to
wash it out before he wakes. My wife starts

humming, Home on the Range, which she'd
sing the kids to sleep with. Mr. Trump's not up

to joining in but contributes some healthy
snoring. I turn off his chirping cellphone.

OLD CHAINSIDES

Not a musky, walleye, or northern pike, just
a lousy pickerel nosing up to the boat behind
my bait—the one usually caught in these waters;
can cause some to lose their minds. Rattling their
chains, the locals say. Just then the sun's covered
by a cloud; the water loses heart; but the wind has
plenty of ideas. Looking down, I suddenly realize

I've had a passion for this fish all along, the way it
shakes the whole lake green like a tremor. When I
bring it in there's my Pop standing on the dock to
see what I've been up to, swearing under his breath,
his bony hand, the coarse fingers angling off, fumbling
with a stringer, in case I've caught something at all
worth keeping, which of course I haven't, never will.

SLATCH

That's the quiet patch between
heavy breakers, just outside

the mouth of a narrow inlet to
the sea. You'd better bide your

time, maneuver just beyond the
rough water, pick a slatch, gun

your boat right through or you'll
be washed to the place where

just a single candle's lit. Amen.

DUNE WILLOW

for STB on Death Row

Even this once abundant shrub on
the sandy shores of Lake Michigan

is going, going, gone now. The one
we always made for at the end of

long, serious walks, shading the little
stream mouthing into the lake north

of town where gulls are fatter than
average, wings everywhere. Some

get out of prison every day, even if
guilty, he says. No big deal. God's not

too disturbed either. I stop talking, pour
us some coffee from the thermos. He

unwraps the sandwiches, breaks his in
half, flings it past a willow that won't

make it. They've got to eat too, he says,
staring at a gull so hard it flies right down.

We shouldn't be so damn greedy. I did
some learning inside, between doobies.

I know enough not to ask what they are,
just nod. I hate dark, confined places . . .

The endless crash of waves on rocks at
our feet is some sort of answer to what's

hanging overhead, about to fall . . .

THE LAST BUTTON

Cupping my hands over theirs,
I drop unseen a button into one

child's hands. The game of course
is to guess who has it. No one knows

it's the last button on my last shirt.
I've been set down in the midst of

a birthday party, asked to come up
with a game all the kids might win.

When I look them up and down, I see
instead of being happy they're about

to quarrel, so I quickly open both fists
to show there's nothing left for me; their

big eyes go teary. It's gotten darker.
Something about a fear in all of us now,

having to catch a glimpse of nothing
in a hand one can't call one's own;

a hand that keeps opening, closing.

SURF FISHING

for Sarah

Actually, I'm just pretending to fish
at Rehoboth Beach. Mostly I'm hoping
to catch sight of her sliding past in
her new blue kayak. She comes here

to recover from treating cancer-kids.
Out on the ocean, she says, she can

let go of some she tried to save. Now,
she's a dot on the horizon, and I wave

at the top of some jumps, but swells
come between us, gray-green waves

cresting to foam, flowing up from deep,
deep trenches, sun going out like a light.

from SPEAK MOUTH TO MOUTH

LATE AT NIGHT

Women swimming in slips, men in long underwear,
a huge fish head washes ashore, its heart and lungs
trailing behind like roots. When we look up, a young
Mexican drowns before we can rush a boat out.

A German doctor tries artificial respiration, but it's
no use, he lies there like a man in a barbershop late
at night, head in the door, getting a shave, his legs
kicking out. He keeps riding the burro till his wife
stops kissing the back of her hand. R.I.P.

LARYNX

Voice box, in front of the windpipe,
just below the hyoid bone, connected
to the pharynx above, the pipe below,

through which every breath of air you
take must pass, but the most exciting
part's the thyroid cartilage, two plates

shaped like sturdy wings which meet
in front of the Adam's apple. Now
imagine getting cancer right there . . .

Better to wake smothered one morning
than to bear testimony to the ugly fight
I've got going with my own cells, Mom

said, whose last words were, I'd not mind
so much if it were only called Eve's apple.
Why would damn Adam get all the words?

BUCK FEVER

Got so excited I couldn't pull the trigger,
the dog tugged loose, Dad turned away.

There goes your only chance, he said,
starting us on the long dusty road to our

vast separation. I squeezed into a corner
of my bed later that night, fearful of making

a sound, a night forever connected to him
pacing back and forth outside my door, his

mouth full of harsh remarks. Finally, he'd say,
How about a nice glass of water? I heard him

swallow it himself when I didn't answer, trudge
back down the stairs, one hard step at a time.

LOOKDOWN

A queer fish to observe coming for your hook.
Mouth down, tail thrown up, body so compact
its profile is anterior, and steep. No scutes along
the lateral line, so if your knife's not sharp, you'll
make a bloody mess of the thin fillets, whose
flesh is pure succulence. Your mother's mouth

waters, she's warming her sick body against
the cleaning shed. Early evening now, you're
both so hungry—once, you were able to do
with less, but then she had to go ahead, get
her cancer. Ever since, nothing but constant
hunger. You look at her, look down, cut in.

BLOOD KNOT

The one drawn up into a roll, two ends
sticking out at right angles to the middle:
said to be the simplest for joining together
any old rope. Simple, hah! I'm still trying
to get it right. Nothing out here but water,
loose ends, no right angle in sight. Been
sitting at the end of the dock a while now,
dangling a foot in little ripples, ice barely
gone, snow still falling, flakes holding out
till they finally dissolve. Waved off supper
a while back. Not coming in till I master
the damn knot, I holler when my father
calls from the cabin, muttering something
about my stubborn streak. We've been
fishing forty years together, a week every
summer, the only time we can find, trying
for friendship past kinship, but these last
few years there's little left but marking
time till he dies, or I do. Accident-prone
as I am, he's made me promise to learn
to tie the knot, still has some patience for
my failures. I give him that, though tonight
seems different. I hear him laugh way out
here. When he laughs louder, I holler, What
about the damn blood, Dad? He's back at
the door in a flash, yells for the world to hear,
That's the thing about the damn knot, till you
get it right, there won't be any left to shed.

OYSTER STEW

No, your mother does pancakes, I do oyster stew
for Sunday brunch, Dad would say when we held
our nose, tapped the pats of butter with our spoons
till he grumbled: All right, you'll never had much of
an educated palate. He dumped the stew outside.
The birds knew what was good for them, at least.

Once, I stopped off for some at The Oyster Bar,
one of those little pints with the wire handle, now
that Mother's dead and Dad's in a nursing home—
at least I can bring him what he wants: he pokes
at the oysters with a crooked finger, They used to
give you an extra couple, he mutters, but can't
get down a spoonful. See these hands, he says,
They could shuck an oyster just like that, didn't
ever use a knife. A queer look flits across his face.

Well, that's how I tried to be with everything, he
goes on after a while. But your mother said I was
too soft. I run a finger over his lips, Remember my
deal with you both, Pop? No getting at each other
through me . . . He holds his breath, but it's no use,
out comes a deep, deep cough: I beg your pardon
Mr. Oldest Son. Just wait till you have a wife you
should have left, who should have left you, too . . .

I wipe his face with a warm cloth. Pop, we're just
glad you stuck together, did the best you could . . .
His eyes close a bit, liquor over like an oyster about
to slide from its shell. It takes some doing to bed him.

WINTER EGGS

Not the water flea's, who carries summer
eggs in a pouch on her back, enclosing
winter ones in murky capsules like earthworms',
filling them with milky fluid spiked with vitamins.

Nor the tiny ones of certain butterflies laid
on stalks, leaves, sometimes water; not oysters',
which can flush millions in a year, so heavy
they sink to the bottom; nor frogs', bubbly,
jellied masses reminding of hilly tapioca.

I mean the ones Gramma's leghorns lay after
she feeds them ear-corn and skim milk—See,
she says, It's the exercise when they peck for
kernels, and the milk's for forming perfect yolks—
eggs so sweet I'd have them sometimes every
meal till I left to eat at other tables, vexed, way

over heels in love, at a loss to see how I could do
anything but return to her farm where the light dawns
right after the first leghorn squawks; and you seize it
by the neck, laugh in its bloody face till she grins.

When I started reading comics in the back
of my uncle's smoke shop, Captain Marvel
said it all the time. So I did too, till Miss Bartz
got after me in class: He only exclaims Holy
Moly when he's really astonished, she said.
I was too stupid to wonder how she knew.

You might not have fallen in love with her,
but I did: those tiny little spectacles perched
atop that sharp nose, a soft blue patch over
one eye, and that long needle of a hairpin
like an arrow running through her hair, not
to forget three chipped front teeth she likely
couldn't afford to have crowned; but I did,

that last day after school ended, when she
stopped in the shop for the biggest cigar we
sold and the new Captain Marvel double issue:
"Please wrap these beautifully," she said, "They're
a birthday gift for my father in the hospital . . ."
I tried to say how sorry I was. "It might please you
to know, young man," she cut me off, "My father
would correct me—'Holy Moses,' he'd shout, 'It's
Holy Moses, give credit where it's due!' I light
father's cigar when Captain Marvel departs for
other crises." With that she pulled on the ribbon
I'd teased out with the scissors so it fluted, tipped
me a shiny quarter, and backed out the door.

BEGGARS' NIGHT

The freedom we have in these helpless costumes!
No more than an earthly, physical sort, but we take
advantage this cold October night, the moon gone.

The idea of knocking on a neighbor's door, freezing
her soul, now that's intelligible pleasure! A brief moment,
to be sure, but full of human tremor. Cocteau put it well:

Children and lunatics cut the Gordian knot, which the rest
of us spend a lifetime trying to untie. For now we're holding
out grab bags, a maneuver for forcing all hands together;

and are seldom refused: the little Mars bar, the two brown
pennies, the bruised apple, all plop down. In the nick of time
we turn: the whole block of porch lights going off as one!

Say you're walking in the woods with your father,
and he's telling you why some trees aren't doing
so well this year. When you ask him for specifics,
because they look fine, in a surly voice the whole
county can hear he suddenly shouts he's tired
of being asked to justify every blooming thing:
Prove it, prove it! As if my life, all my experience
amounted to a hill of bad beans. He's talking
way down low, now. You hear some real panic
to how he's been challenged, again and again
over the years. Think I'll strike out for the woods,
you recall he'd say, stomp out, slink back later.

So you kneel down, grab some dirt, bounce on
your haunches, trying to make yourself a child;
but when you reach out to take his hand, he pulls
it away in disgust. Maybe it's the moment to give
give up any idea of ever making peace again.

See that blue ash over there? You point. Suppose
it's going to die soon, is that what you'd say, Dad?

What are you blabbing about, he says, striding past
you: You're drunk, boy look out now! He totters over,
rolls into a ball. Like a drunk you do too, smack up
against his back, take his hand without a word . . .

Ever going to believe anything I say, Pa? he stammers.
Sure, son, sure, you say, touching your head to his. Soon
as you wake up with the truth on your lips, sure I will . . .
       You're bawling and babbling now.

THE CROSS AND THE KISS

Remember when we couldn't read or write?
Just make a cross, right here, someone said,
related to the king. Now kiss it the way you
would your grandma's Bible, so we know
you're behind us all the way. He left and we
went back to our awkward gestures of love.

These days, the steady thunder of our pens
and pencils would make our ancestors think
of mountains falling down. When I kiss you
I'd like intimacy; but for now, separate as
we are, these little *xxxes,* curiously quiet,
will have to do instead. They reach your
eyes which, under those black lashes, keep
my cry in the darkness alive, and nothing
else of your face can be seen for tears.

LONESOME WATER

Drink it and back you go, sometimes
as far as your childhood home, to die.
Gravels clear it, willows dapple it, while
thoughts turn to changes for the worse.

It's more and more possible for your
parents to bring evidence against you.
They dance around your crib, pull at
your flesh, crack nasty jokes in a state
of near frenzy. Will it be over soon,

you plead, your voice running down,
your fever spiking. Maybe they are
in love with you in their own fashion,
maybe they're merely saving you from
awful secrets, you think at last, while

in the woods the stream's filling with
water again after years of drought.

GIRAFFE

A neck of only seven bones, like the lowly mouse.
Legs all the same length, even though you'd swear

the hind ones are shorter. Keen smell and sight
(beautiful eyes!). Can outrun most predators, but

once overtaken is easily killed, alas. Quite a piece
of work, all in all; but can you imagine having no

voice, not being able to utter the slightest sound,
even in extreme danger? Numbed by fear, even

a child can cry. Rearing, plunging, backing, side-
stepping, a few last flings before planting all

four hooves to brace for the lion's last lunge.
Watching from afar, our hearts sink, but our

screams rise; and down we look to drown our
sorrow, while the giraffe swallows its tongue.

DEATH GLOW

It's winter but there's thunder.
Dad's doctor knocks and enters
before I blurt, Yes? Off he goes
to draw the drapes, when I stop
him: Can you please give Dad
more morphine? It can't be long
now, and he's struggling. Don't
worry, we won't accuse you of
addicting him. Doc's not amused,
and motioning to the nurse steps
into the hall. I hear them argue.

When I go to moisten Dad's lips,
his eyes brighten, cheeks flush;
and for a moment I think, he'll
pull through, but of course he
doesn't. That rattle starts up
between phrases, long pauses,
and the constant turn of his head.
I fall asleep. He's dead when I wake.

ON CRADLES

for Betsy

Earliest ones, we're told, were hewn from
half-logs that swayed and rolled, baby tied
down with dark leather thongs, rocked by
Mama's foot, who sat working, humming
first lullabies; pine cones tucked in as toys.

Moses, any Bible will tell you, was set off in
a papyrus basket plastered with pitch, which
luckily didn't have to double as a tiny boat.
What would the Nile have cast its way?

Anthropologists say first Laplanders swung
their babes in hammocks lined with seal fur.
Fastening them to walrus tusks, they stuck
them in their hut's icy walls, clapped until
the wind did its job, and sleep could come
to all, the reindeer crowding in around.

From the size of Henry VIII's, you can see
why he'd eventually go crazy over things:
the contraption had a hooded cowl that
could be raised for sun and smiles, lowered
for cries and scowls. A different model, who
knows, Anne might have lived a normal life.

Prosperous early Americans covered theirs
with several leathers and intricate patterns
of brass nails. Ben Franklin's said to have tried
a simpler design, but turned to lightning
instead, while Tom Paine fed his to the fire
in one of those terrible winters fit for no soul.

Friends in Florence have had one in the family
since 1713. Their daughter dons a Communion
frock to rock her dolly in it, while I read her
favorite Bible stories and stare hard at I.H.S.
carved deeply into the headboard. Christ is
a new experience for me at this low level.

Our son in Zurich in the Sixties, having been
scolded on a playground for sticking a finger
into the fountain—That's for birds, someone's
nanny shrieked—climbed into his sister's and
bunged his mouth with thumb. We used little
knobs on the sides to tie him safely inside.

The one out the window today, of fine grass,
lined with lichens and milkweed floss, must be
a hummingbird's, not trusting to beady others.

142

ERYSIPELOID

An infection, which often starts when a fishbone
punctures your finger. Swelling and a purplish
discoloration soon set in, spread to your hand,
and on down to the tip of the adjoining finger.

Blood poisoning set in the last time it happened,
so this time I dropped everything, headed for
the clinic in Nonesuch, near the Kentucky lake
I'd been cleaning out, catching way too many

spawning bass defending their nests, sometimes
the same one over and over for the stupid thrill
of hauling in a whopper, when it finally hit me:
Enough already! my Dad would say, How much

can you eat, anyway? The last time we fished
together, the sky beginning to pale in the late
afternoon light, I'd disagree as usual. We were
good at spending whole days arguing, then;

looking at each other with a peculiar impatience,
Mom imploring us to grow up, pretending to leave.
Forty years of fishing together, not finding any joy,
but now that he's gone I'm frightened, can't find

it alone. Easing the hook out as gently as possible,
cradling the bass in my cold hands, I was about to
slip it back into the lake when it suddenly twisted.
"Leave the wound open," doc said, after the shot.

ON GETTING VERY SICK
IN A FOREIGN COUNTRY
AND BEATING IT THE HELL HOME

1 *Trying to remember the painting you loved,*
you fall down the museum steps, break a leg

She who was once the helmet maker's beautiful wife
is now your nurse. "Please strip to socks and shoes, Sir,"
she says. "Put this on, it ties in back. We'll give you
something to put you half asleep. It'll dry your mouth;
you allergic to anything at all?"
"No, no, I like them all," you cry, lie down on a gurney,
get rolled into a tiny, dark office. Cleaning his ears with
a Q-tip, a doctor dressed in a naval uniform shakes your
hand. You notice he has dirty fingernails.

2 *Town square: people and cars milling around*

Like going for a ride in the dark: just as you recall
you've eaten something disagreeable, a black
Citröen stops. A man inside hands you a bunch
of radishes. You tear one off, pop it in your mouth:
suddenly, there's pain; you forget how to walk, fall
off the curb. The car's window slowly rolls up.

3 *Dusty room at night*

"The baby in the basket's gone!" the woman beside
you cries. Just a woman on a burro. Get a woman on
a burro in your mind, hope the burro's not on top; any
woman, holding a child's hand, a bundle on her head.
It should be a woman coming out a pink door, waiting
for a bus with a gold star on its side; going from Here to
There: "Please, not too many stitches, Captain Doctor
of the Clean Ears! And a receipt so I can be reimbursed
by my miserable insurance." He is seemingly amused.

4 *Hysteria sets in*

I had diarrhea, trouble breathing, couldn't sleep;
a pin of a pain in my chest. My back, my foot ached;
and now I'm constipated, can you direct me to an open
apothecary? But more than anything, are all my meals
included? I don't know how to take these pills, please
speak more slowly. Something's the matter in my head.
Excuse me, officer , what time is it? My watch won't wind!

5 *Reading Kafka on the train from Prague to Vienna*

He smiles, doesn't seem to give a damn. I can't stop him,
which I regret. I like my Swiss watch, it's so expensive, but
I just don't trust it, and am led before a magistrate. "Your
Honor, Sir, what time is it now, please? Time to leave yet?"

6 BACK HOME

A nice family in a small town near Plum Creek. A comfortable
old red brick house that just needs a little work; on the gutters,
the masonry, you name it. Oh, and a way to keep the pigeons
off the window ledges; and a rusty car in the driveway, so I can
climb in the back seat, close windows before lightning strikes.

"Pink is as pink supposes," said
Gertrude Stein late one afternoon,
just before dusk. In France, of course,
with Mr. Hemingway coming over for
something to drink, work to show,
advice to get, but we can't be sure.

"I will tell you YES. YES! Yes yes yes.
Yes AH yesssss, most certainly YESSS!
Mr. Hemingway," I imagine she said;
"And I will tell you NOOO, oh my Lord
NO," maybe even NOPE, nosireesir, No!
And then you must go home, figure out
the difference," is what I hope she finally
offered to do for him, more or less . . .

Some birds came along over drinks, and
Alice may have said, "It's too early for
ravens; they're sure to be waxwings."
"Who cares?" Gertrude would sigh, "As
long as Mr. Hemingway won't shoot them."

The sky dark, the last waxwing, petrified,
let the end of its pink ribbon slip to its breast,
then tugged hard to noose its scrawny neck.

NUNS FISHING

for Barbara

For what, may I ask, when I pass by
along the shore of the shallow bay,

careful to seem politely nonchalant,
not to stare at the little black crosses

nestled against their soft white robes,
their faces as one in the setting sun.

Without taking her eye off her bobber,
one says with something of a lisp, "Just

the John Dory, the fish with that black
spot Saint Peter's thumbprint left when

he took a coin from its mouth." "God
save us from His secrets," I try, which

prompts her to put down her pole,
slowly approaches me, a fixed look

in her black eyes. "I thought you weren't
coming," she says at last, as if I'd been

expected for years. "Yes, well, here I am,
go on please," I say. Suddenly, the other

nuns reel in their lines, leave the two of us
standing there, breathing the air between.

"My fishing years are past," I finally manage
to whisper. "Yes, yes, I know," she nods, "it's

like being without sunlight when Father's away."
I draw crosses in the sand, her tears in my eyes.

ZAUNKÖNIG

What the Germans called a new torpedo in
their arsenal, "fitted with a listening device

so it homed onto sounds of ships' propellers."
The Brits called it "gnat," and there you have

the difference in their minds: German for "wren,"
the perfect English word for the tough little bird,

while "Zaun" (fence) and "König (king), as you
can see, quite aside from ignoring many other

birds that light on fences, goes poetical to put it
badly, which reminds me of Mozartian melodies

German pilots listened to on London bombing runs.
When I listen to Amadeus these days, I pull my cap

over my ears, clamber into the little cockpit of our
car, and tootle off in no hurry toward town: not

a wren in sight on the fences, most of which need
new slats and paint. Now and then, a goshawk

drops down out of the drowsy sky, something to eat
wriggling in its talons. Politely, it turns its back to dig in,

shows a yawn as if to say, See, nice and clean now, no
rubble below, soon takes flight again, growing smaller.

ZITRONENCREME

for Sylva

The lemon mousse after the Christmas goose:
back in 1933 it was, when after baptized Jews

blew out the candles on the tree and led their
children to the Christmas feast, servants left to

pitch a bucket of water at wayward candles.
Blessings were said, hopes were high "the storm"

would blow over, but it wouldn't. Grampa talked
and talked till Gramma flew at him, seized him by

a sleeve. When Uncle Julius disappeared, even
the children knew they'd best draw caps down

over their brows, not repeat a syllable of talk they
heard. "Lord, how afraid they must have been,"

Mother took to saying when she sliced the brisket
for Sunday meals in Milwaukee in the weeks after

the war. I've since asked myself if hugs and tears
kept most of the family from fleeing Senice, even

after Great-gramma Fanny was murdered at 102:
in the album she's wiping her hands on her apron

before walking proudly out to face the flock of SS
in the yard, pecking away at the icing on the mousse.

FLOATING HEART

Loves a shallow pond, spreads
its tiny white flowers over broad

leaves; and proceeds till it covers
the whole surface, sometimes in just

one summer. If you're foolish enough
to turn it over, look for the heart,

legend has it you'll not only not
catch the pickerel lurking below,

you'll quarrel with those you love,
cry yourself to sleep with worry; and

in the morning head nude and cold for
the old rowboat tied to a stump; climb

aboard, paddle quickly out to the middle,
then float slowly back ashore in a wooden

coffin, when the pickerel goes belly up.

DOCK SPIDER

She's hung her egg sac in the corner of
the tire bumper at the end of the dock.

By the time I tie up after a hard day's
fishing, I see she's down a leg already.

Who knows where it ended up? But she uses
the other seven, elaborate ebony chopsticks,

to fork water striders skimming the lake's
surface right under her web. She's stretched

out so flat and black you can't see her for
the tire at first, but oh how you gasp when

I pull you down on a knee to point her out!
I'm not about to pretend I'm not horror-struck

as well: she'd be a match for a baby octopus.
Chris, the dockhand, who knows these things,

says she's on the way to dying, having done
her job; and will soon position herself so that

her hatching babies won't miss their first
meal, by which time she'll be liquefying.

I mumble something about mama's milk, but
you say she should be called the Jesus spider.

For days we force ourselves to follow nature's
little drama as the egg sac quivers, while she

barely moves an inch away, ignoring anything
her web traps. On our last night, gunning back

before a sudden storm, scrambling to secure
the canoe, we almost forget to have a look

when you pull me down beside you. At first,
there's nothing to see so we lean way over.

The tire's corner pocket is ablaze with scads
of tiny pearly white bodies who've eaten well.

We don't linger over dinner, our glasses going
quickly up to our mouths, coming down empty.

KNAUTSCHKE

for Anette & Thomas

Obaysch, the first hippo to reach Europe
since Roman times, inspired the "Hippo Polka,"
which my parents kept alive in Milwaukee at
the Steuben Society Social till WW II ended,
when they learned of Knautschke, one of
a few survivors in Berlin's fabled zoo.

"At least God," Mom said, "has vouchsafed him
more life." I promised to pay respects when I went
off in 1949 as an exchange student, took a cheap
room near what was left of the zoo. When I could,
I'd sit on a bench watching Knautschke keep his act
going for the pitiful few who took a break from surviving
for a little stroll past his sad island. For an hour or so,
he'd nose a large, scarred wooden block, which
seemed fallen from a bombed building, gingerly up
out of the moat, almost to the top of his compound
before nonchalantly circling it, pausing to look us
over, before he sent it plunging back down into
the muddy water as an afterthought, and an old
woman, bracing herself on two canes, hollered,
"That's an animal who'd find God if He existed."

MOONLIGHT'S

Bad for you if you're a tiny critter
whose predators can spot you nights,

smashing twigs that come between,
their teeth itching to kiss your neck.

They've no business there, you might
have thought if you could think at all,

following them with your eyes, the way
my uncle's eyes followed the torpedo

surging along the moonlit alley between
the Japanese sub and his freighter, chest

rattling, lips freezing till all grew quiet as
the fish missed, only the lapping waves

and someone aft playing a harmonica in
a gloomy frame of mind. When my uncle

taught me how to drive right after the war,
in his new coupe bought with severance pay,

he said before he let me turn the key: "Always
remember, kid, cars are really mean killers."

We were out under some moon, the light
of those slain draining from our eyes.

THANK THE ONE ABOVE

1

Nominal Jews like me, never past secular,
love Catholics, Catholic women in particular,
Christmas trees too (I trim a nifty one), &
pork of course, among other telling markers.

We donate regularly to Catholic charities
(known to keep administrative costs down).
When my wife's subscription lapsed, I leapt
to renew *Commonweal* in my name, look

forward to cheffing for her new priest when
it's time to have him over. Father Frank, retired,
didn't care what I served so long as we had
Boodles gin on hand, waved aside my pitiful

efforts to shake a proper martini, just poured
a healthy jigger down some ice cubes, never
mind the vermouth. "How bout them apples?"
he winked, since become my go-to mantra

for just-do-it situations. Now that the new priest
not only condones my decision to donate my
body to the local med school, adds the act's
heartily endorsed by The Church, I'm thinking

of looking into RCIA sessions. But I don't dare
mention my intention in public anymore after
my old pal blanched, way too upset: "Thanks
for guaranteeing I see just your cadaver from

now on, damn you . . . And my wife, who's been
leaning toward gifting her remains, has enjoined
me from blabbing it, especially at the P.O., where
I do time every day, love telling anyone in line

I ask for my own window at Christmas, but never
get it. As for blabbing, I admit I told my daughter,
whose own Anatomy 101 cadaver I got to meet.
I wanted her approval most of all; been turning

to her more & more, not just when I wake scared
& sweating some darker nights. She's careful as
an angler releasing an under-size fish, so I get to
swim back to notions of what it might be like to

kneel at the altar, close eyes, stick out my tongue,
while what's left of the presentimental Jew in me
waits for some word from The One Above. Gramma
said NEVER EVER say the G-word unless you're willing

to sleep in your old bed, the room empty save for
your old rabbi behind his enormous desk, pulling
his beard out when you wailed, But I don't want
to read or write right to left, I only stalked Harlene

Harberg home from Hebrew School to see if she
was going to survive the after-effects of her beauty
& fall for me before the pendulum fell off the clock.

2

Been lately hard to resist the temptation to taste
Communion, especially for the cook in me who's
got to sample whatever I dish out. When Mother
stuck her tongue out for a bit of mac & cheese—

I was feeding her at The Jewish Home for the Aged—
little white spots made me drop the spoon. "Don't
come back till you've gotten past revulsion," she
whispered, "I'll be here till I'm no longer wanted."

You could see she was a great Latinist in school,
said she'd have married Cicero if only he'd stuck
around. I'm looking at her old report cards now,
a string of 99s for eight terms of Latin, high marks too

for math—no wonder she loved helping me with
algebra—but average grades in everything else,

especially typing, which she skipped to sunburn
at the beach. Alas, never asked her about her
own religious leanings, though of all the Garbers
she seemed the most spiritual, flew at the rabbi

who had it in for me, seized him by the sleeve,
raised her voice to a level I'd never heard, "My
son is impulsive but not argumentative!" "So?"
is all he said in an agitated voice, & that did it.

Saturdays from then on free for sandlot football,
till I broke my nose and needed more than sulfa,
the first lot to be made public near war's end.
Dr. Schwartz, an old Navy man, tapped sources

to get me enough to not die. His good wife came
by daily during her hospital ministry, politely asking
if she could pray over me, let me fondle her rosary.
The next day she brought me my very own, said to

work the beads as if making a necklace for Mother
for Christmas, left me singing "Fall On Your Knees, O

Hear the Angel Voices, O Christ" something or other.
I slipped back under, seized by a hand in a dream.

Christ opened it, put something in, closed it again.
"What's the matter?" mother said when I woke up
sweating. "Need time to think things over, please!"

3

Ever since, that moment's meant more & more time
to do nothing but while away more time. Mother lit
another cigarette, let me blow the match out. She's
been long gone, she who could solve many a painful

equation of my relationships, sitting silently by, sipping
her Blatz, while I drew little Vs. Birds flocking, I said when
the page was full, toward God. "Here, take a little more
tapioca," she'd coo, my favorite comfort food. "How

can he stomach those little fish eyes," father would say
when he came home from "making a living so you'll
have it better." He'd changed his name from Immanuel
so his customers wouldn't know you-know-what. More

than once I heard him swallow hard when guys said kike
and the like. But for him I'd not have learned how to hook
muskys, filet them just right for Gramma's gefilte fish. Both
of us stopped short of total indifference to each other.

He'd understand, if mistakenly, why I'd go Catholic now,
curse everyone else for making it inevitable, trudge off
into the woods to shoot another deer to dress, but stamp
back clenching fists if he missed a shot. When he lay dying,

refusing to rehab a broken hip, I tried cursing him, hoping
his bile would boil up again; caught myself in shameful
thoughts, how did I know reformation would set in? "I'll
miss you some" is all he said, closed one eye and died.

As if everything would be all right, I plopped down beside
him, snugging our bodies, "He won't do it again" ringing
in my ears when mother once begged him—for Christ's
sake—not to take a belt to me. I'd been building Zeros

on his workbench without permission, stupidly left a mess
behind, compounding his anger. I loved Zeros for their
markings, even though they were shooting at my uncle
off to war on an atoll who knew where. Dad just missed

having been inducted, so that must have had something
to do with it. Huddling for the Kaltenborn news at supper,
when it looked like we might lose at first, we all OYed in
chorus, I crossed myself, learned from Georgie Karjanis

on the corner, so fast no one noticed. Better take Ambien
now, get some sleep so I won't bite my cheek till it bleeds,
have come close to buying a restrainer to stop gnashing.
If you were bedside, looked at me, you'd call 911. As for

being a really good prospect for converting, I feel naked
as a slave praising the Lord. Afraid of the next cloudburst.
Not how one should live, unless training an army to die.
High time to bury indulgencies. First scissor them up, then

collage into a target behind the bar in the basement. New
Year's down there, friends & family droning in and out, vats
of boiling shrimp, washing them down with Bloody Marys.

Sharpened darts on Dad's old lathe till he banged my back,
snatched them away. "Here, Mr. Know-It-All, I'll show you how
to hunt!" Never saw so many bulls-eyes! Which blurt earned
a pat on my head, a faint sign I might amount to something

after all. Well, I'll leave you now, more excitement's bad for
the heart I've heard. Have to think about supper, consolation
in the bracing Catholic company of my wife, more and more
the reason life's easier. Though we seldom see eye to eye,

she's always been willing to taste if not eat all of what I dish
up, on stoneware we've yet to wear down to its elements.
The candle lit, the dark coming down. We can just make out
the last of the birds at the feeder, always a female cardinal,

and a downy male woodpecker hanging upside down from
the suet staked on top, no more cross-bills to make their life
miserable. Raising our glasses, we say a little prayer I learned
in Germany from the old Catholic innkeeper, when away so

long I got so homesick if I hadn't bailed out of a translation
project, high-tailed it back to Ohio, who knows what . . . "Bread
from wheat, wheat from light, light from the sight of God."

from ON THE BOTTOM

PROXIMODISTAL

Meaning the fetus develops from the minuscule,
elongated mass of cells along the neural groove,

which morphs into a spinal column if all goes well.
When we provide assistance the next ever so many

years, is that nothing? I'm walking in the garden with
my daughter, trying to explain why the bushes aren't

doing well. She bends to wattle them with her fingers;
such a quiet little girl, her hair sticking to her temples.

We know she has thoughts and feelings we can't sense
yet, if ever. Suddenly, she catches a butterfly I'd not seen,

its wings powdering her palms. I want to say, Please let it
go, but her eyes dwell on it with such tenderness I know

it'll spread its wings wide again soon. Well, she says, putting
it back on a leaf, I'd like to play tea-time now, pulls me back

toward the house. I ought to tell her, I . . . She goes quicker &
quicker, while I long to rest, go slower & slower, scared now,

rub my chest, lose my balance till she graduates from med
school and gives me a stethoscope for listening to the past.

MADONNAS

1 *Portrait Madonnas*

She usually appears half-length against solid
gold leaf, cherubs around her blue robe starred
in turn with gold, draped over her quiet head.

In Italy's oldest churches, she's dark and fair,
as tall as you, but like women who've never
worked, there's a melancholy over her brow,
as if she'd dread giving birth again; but then
there's that moment, her eyes looking away,
a door perhaps ajar at the end of a long hall,
God's head about to overwhelm the opening.

2 *Madonna Enthroned*

She's sitting on a throne with harpies or saints
around her, never both. I can't look, she seems
to say, turning a hand round and round as if
in a trance. Her cheeks have lost some bloom.

If the Devil appeared, she'd climb right down,
run to God. "But we're the family of—the boy,"
she'd plead. "And it's your place to protect us!"
A faint doubt crosses her eyes, "Were we doing
right?" she wonders. "Let him take my place, no
one will miss me." A feverish wind blows through.

3 *Madonna in the Sky*

It's like starting a new life up there, living in a bigger
house, Heaven a halo of light, clouds floating round.

A bit above, some cherubs seem to be carrying on.
In the earliest paintings, the Glory is nicely oval, but
her eyes seem empty, as if she were glad to be out
of sight, would be relieved if we only looked away.

4 *Pastoral Madonna*

As you'd expect, the background's pure landscape,
sometimes just bare rocks or roses, though more often
there's quite a garden & she's the gardener, wrought-
iron shears at her belt. Scent in the air, that mysterious
aid to memory, revives you. But what's this, in the little
frame in the hall of the inn, she's talking to an angel
who seems concerned about a scratch on her face!
I wash my hands—through the window over the sink,
there's a steep stone wall rising over the Rhone valley.

5 *Madonna in the House*

The fewest in number, by Northern painters who were
happiest at home, it seems. Look, there she is in some
Flemish bedroom, nothing much to tell you of her life.
And there, at the carpenter's, a knot in a string around
her finger, her rosary of tiny beads crying out, "May
the Holy Ghost be with you!" In another, she's gossiping
about Jesus to a neighbor, "He'll be coming home soon,
muddy no doubt, I better fix his supper." And in one we
own, over the bed in the back bedroom, she's helping
herself to the one perfect chocolate in a dirty brown box.
"We're either going up to Bethlehem next season, or down
to the seashore to watch the men cast their nets for fish,"
she seems to be saying, "But I just don't know for sure."

SOME SUN ON CLOUD TOPS

For some, Hopper-minded, an image
of extreme loneliness. For me, a sign

to sharpen dull hooks, drink at least two
Labatts and appear well pleased even if

I'm weeks into cabining on this tiny island,
the fishing the poorest in many a summer,

the blueberries late so the bears are coming
closer, the last golden eagle overhead unable

to scare the flock of gulls off far enough for
its customarily larger share of fry, both eyes

squeezed in as if to say, *I'm to blame, relax.*
So I do before heading down to bail the boat

out, yank the cord hard, start the balky Evinrude.
Loon Lake's perfect in the half-shade, the sun

mercifully deciding to stay hidden just enough
to keep the water murky with dark clouds, wind

chopping the surface so nothing alive below can
see me casting to structure. Hopper, I read, liked to

fish alone, too. He'd camp at the end of the dock,
gnawing a blade of grass, the sun starting to fleck

the wall of his cabin, whose single window a solitary
female figure leaned out of, unwilling to wave to him.

COURTSHIP

A mere speck at first, the male eagle you've been watching
suddenly dives down on a female skimming the water past

the birches lining the shore. You're in the lodge's old yellow
canoe, I'm in a pram fishing off your bow without any luck,

when suddenly you're pointing with your paddle, hollering.
I drop my rod to see what you see: the last second before

he's on her; she flips to her back, they lock talons, roll over
and over till we grow dizzy, lock grins before drifting apart.

You put in at a little cove, hunt for blueberries the bears
have missed, while I motor off to my bass hole for the main

course of our nightly repast. Half a century we've come here
summers, up on the Canadian shield, happy as we've ever

been, on the other side of rough waters you've seen me through,
more than Loon Lake can toss up. If you ever need a tow back

the rope's coiled at my feet, though with your skills you play
the wind just right, are back at the dock when I putt-putt in.

MOTHER, FISHING

We'd fluke along, driven by
the way she worked the oars,
as if she owned the whole lake.

I've seen water good as dead
brought back to life with her
rowing. If I could, I'd work

every blooming day like that,
even Sundays, until everyone
would see that things were

right—I'm blurting, excuse me,
but she's dead and gone, one
year to this August day out on

High Lake. Will we ever see
the musky she was after near
the end, the kind of fish whose

flesh won't go from greater
to less, is even too strong for
gefilte fish? I've left the shore

behind, with the repose of
a mother who'd close her eye
before tying into one: Now

this is a whale of a fish, she'd
yell, And it's moving in with us,
make room! Waving off the net

I'd scramble for, she settled back
on her torn cushion, whispering,
Before I took over, your father

was doing all right, you know.
Now hand me the pliers, the hook's
gone down too far. No glory in that.

THIRD & GALENA

In memory of Herb Blau

The Italians were Dagos, the Frenchies Frogs,
we were plain old Yids, and the Polish Umpkes
supplied us all with cabbage rolls stuffed with
ground pork and rice, especially Augie's mom's.

After he'd muss me up for stealing just a pack
of Wings from my pop's drugstore, he'd let me
have a drag, touch the Captain Richard Bong
card from the back of the pack, claiming he

was the first Ace of Polish descent. You wouldn't
want to disagree, and I'd get to eat at his house
where we'd polish off *galumpkis* as if they were
just so many Twinkies, and Mrs. Malowski sent me

home with a dozen more. Augie's dead & gone
now, there's no reason to attend another reunion,
the only time I could beat him at arm wrestling.
By then he knew Bong had Swedish blood, but

I didn't rub it in. After too many brews, we'd slip
into the alley behind school, hide in the hollyhock
patch, pull out Luckies, poor cousins of Wings, we
joked. Augie still carried Bong's card in his wallet,

whom we saluted before heading back for the last
festivities, at which the emcee, usually Freddie Fox,
would have the spotlight directed at us, shout out,
"There's America for you, folks, a Yid and an Umpke,

still friends no matter what!" Augie started coughing,
and I'd join him for solidarity until his lungs stopped
working. He'd stagger, all grew dark, something fell.
The Chinese lanterns couldn't keep the light alive.

HALLUX

The reversed toe that lets perching birds
grip a branch, I read. Would the plural be

halices, I ask my funny old high school
Latin teacher in a dream, whom we said

awful things about in recess. Her eyes flash,
she puts her hands to her head, straightening

her hair, removing something like a knitting
needle to point at our stupid faces, "Ah, you

miserable prisoners!" Her admonishing finger
gets me to her side quicker than I know I can run.

"When I leave you to your empty devices, void
and desolate of counsel," she sinks into reverie,

"I take several streetcars and one bus until I am
back with my peregrine falcon at my farmhouse.

If you don't fail me, I shall let you pet her some day
before I send her sky-high so she can show you why

she's the fastest bird in the skies." She kept me by
the force of her grip from thinking anything but.

COUGARS KILL PEOPLE

But prefer children, I say, killing the usual family gossip
—who's on or off the wagon again, who's bi-polaring,
abusing meds, losing tons in the market—it's the annual
Thanksgiving get-together at Aunt Jessie's. We all have
kids, just about the only thing we still have in common.

Uncle Oliver finally says, spinning the ice in his glass,
"Where?" Like an echo, I say "Where?" Aunt Bea pipes
up, "You're in one of your melancholy moods, keep it up
and you'll drive me to drink even more." "We're not at
the point yet of having drunk enough to stupefy us,"

Cousin Ethel tosses over her shoulder, on the way for
a refill. Leaning against the bookcase, Gramma Anna
suddenly opens what looks like a bible. "For those whose
hands are defiled by blood; Isaiah: 2-11," she warbles.
Down from the U.P., distant cousin Max demands I

supply the exact reference, starts yelling I read too many
books for bits to interject when I don't like the drift, jumps
up from the couch, sticks his jaw out. He's a big dude with
an unhealthy complexion, a milkman who once found me
under his horse and slapped the hell out of me. No one

was in time to stop him. As for me, I'm beginning to forget
where I read most anything, think I might even be making
stuff up. And think of running away when I start to blabber.
Well, there we all are, waiting for Grampa Izzie to die, who's
in the back bedroom, so we can put a clove in his hairy nose.

He's the only one of us who's ever seen anything remotely
like a cougar, somewhere in the Carpathians, quickly got
out of the way when it leapt out of the woods, and would
act both parts when we were impressionable, and begged.

"LARGE STURGEON CAUGHT WITH IRON CROSS IN STOMACH"

So ran a headline in 1927; turns out
a WW I German soldier, despondent,
jumped into a river and drowned.

No one took notice of the fisherman,
a long-gone cousin of Erich, a pal from
exchange-student days, who rigged up

some sort of metronome to practice
piano by. Turning a score's pages, I'd
sit beside him till his mother called us

to raspberries & cream. She'd steer us
around "shameful thoughts" of the war
with such tenderness we'd stop short of

darker worries. "That was our way," she'd
always end up saying, "Though not God's."
Having translated German poets for years,

who didn't choose exile, who may have
"contributed," some Commissions put it,
I only know I'd also have taken fright,

not drawn myself up to my full height in
like circumstances. Would you have, well?

PRECIPITAZIONE DALL'ALTO

Fall from a high perch, that is, as noted in
official documents, which brings to mind

Primo Levi's death in clubs and spades. After
lasagna we hurry to see the stairwell he jumped

into, or fell as some have posited. Looking up,
we wish him still standing behind the banister,

perhaps not sure what to do next, frozen by
remorse, if that's what engulfed him; but he's

not & for a quarter of a century now we've tried
living as quietly and peacefully as possible, you

attending Mass wherever available, I thinking
about converting; much more impatient, vile

images coming over me at times, clenching fists
now and then, rarely able to keep my muttering

private. "Come!" You manage to shake me free,
"Let's drink something to his memory, decide to

donate our bodies to research," which means of
course we must not suffer a violent death, the form

warns, or die of anything communicable. Reading
the fine print, I blanch: "One may donate one's eyes,

but nothing else," and hand over the clinic's manual.
"That'll do for now," you whisper, "if not end the tale."

BRIEF REFLECTION ON
THE BLACK 6 MOUSE

One dreary Prague morning, everyone wall-eyed,
Russian tanks still circling the crumbling Clinic for

Experimental Medicine, Dr. Holub introduced me to
his "silly poetic pals," a special strain of nude mice,

which his Russian assistant, who'd often forget to wash
her hands, doom ongoing experiments, padded in with

—a new generation in their little tray, buried under wood-
shavings, dozens of beady eyes protruding. Fingering a tail,

he pulled one up, swung it back & forth, put it on my arm
before coaxing it down into his palm, reminding me of my

grandmother making a mouse from a big kerchief, popping
it along her arm by flexing her muscles. I felt its skin, rubbery

like a rhino's I once touched. Then it hit! Where's the fur?
Something we know by one skin, in another. Something

so fetal, I looked around for a tube to slide it in. When Dr.
Holub was called to the phone, he left me with the tray.

As if my life depended on it, I fed the whole lot tidbits from
a jar, providing like a mother. "What are you DOING, that's

unsterile food! It will ruin our data, Dr. Holub shouted when he
returned, which brought his assistant running. "But Professor,"

her voice dimmed, "What difference does it make? No one cares anymore . . ." His head drooped. "Well, then, might

as well pet them too," he shrugged. "Let's try to visit Kafka's grave now, he'll be eager to know all's still quite normal."

What Jews accused of raising grain prices in Germany
in 1816 were called, "the year without a summer," I read.
So what else is new? The old man ate his gruel, the old
woman licked her bowl clean, but only after she ground
her teeth and he clenched his fists, while we sometimes
still weep, our faith no answer for much of anything these
dreary days, absent peace among the usual adversaries.

Time for less silence, our Israeli cousins finally wrote, along
with a tinny CD of their youngest practicing to play like
Horowitz, they joked. When I knocked, after decades of
nothing between us, our common language German
because I bailed out of Hebrew school, their Yiddish
morphing into German between deep sighs, we sat
circled around little Esther, pecking away at the keys.

Wired to everyone alive in Israel, Abba Kovner made
just two calls when he deciphered the Hebrew fragment
on the "precious" postcard from Mom's long lost cousins
we thought murdered, which she'd sent me off with to
hunt for them. Cousin Max, Esther's father, tipped his
jigger to toast the new rye harvest, the grain that can
poison you if it's not detoxified. We ate our fill, moving
from table to stove and back, all through the night.

NEW POEMS

HEAVEN OR HELL: YOUR CHOICE!

the sign along 511 to Kipton says,
where I bike to lunch in the gazebo
near the old granary, its windows
mostly broken so birds fly in & out.

The old depot's gone now, but you
may know about "The Great Kipton
Train Wreck" of 1891; the expression
"on the ball" too, for which we can

thank Webb Ball, the plaque reads,
a jeweler investigating time & watch
conditions throughout the Lake Shore
& Michigan Southern Railway lines,

who designed a time-keeping program
& watches trainmen still use, after he
concluded one engineer's watch was
"possibly four minutes slow!" #14, a fast

mail train, had collided with the Toledo
Express. (Hell came way too fast for nine
souls who died, but let's hope Heaven's
where they flew to.) Google Curator &

historian Nancy Pope for the grisly details.
Then come sit here to watch the birds cut
collages out of the sweet summer air, kids
swinging on the little playground adjacent,

voices pitched to shrieks at times shrouding
any groans & moans left over from that April

day cars were "telescoped and smashed
to kindling wood, and one rolled over on

the station platform, breaking the depot's
windows." Suddenly, my mouth parches,
I can't finish my sandwich, break it to bits
to toss to the birds, one of which ventures

close enough to pet, chirping agreeably.
God was with you, too, I whistle, as if it had
escaped from the cage a little girl held on
her lap in the parlor car before colliding with

#14; a little girl of auburn hair, tiny teardrops
in her eyes, unexpectedly hurtled towards
an awful exclamation, her mother shot off
in another direction, no time to choose be-

tween Heaven or Hell. Well, what's done is
done, but suddenly amid the dead silence
now, you might find it hard to stoop down
at the little spigot the playground kids can't

turn back on quickly enough to slake each
other's thirst, and from somewhere a little
bird, screeching, petrifies in the stony sky.

WHAT'S FOR DINNER? WILDERNESS?

Large red signs along Washington's 101 read,
protesting the expansion of a national park.
Even morons strung out on stuff will regain
consciousness by the third day, beg for food.

Some of us resort to scornful laughter, even
cynical abuse at such lunacy, which is no
match for the zeal of the single-minded, who
propagate like nettles in this land of the free.

I admit to being preoccupied with my own
affairs to do more than curse, too cowardly
even to stop, at least try to deface a sign or
two: hah, as if that'd even make me wiser.

At a lookout's roadhouse I sample a few local
brews, but can't even cry in them. If you're an
experienced doctor, I'm an experienced patient,
someone says somewhere in Dostoevsky, then

downs a glass to the end of the affair. "Money
puts everything right," the guy next to me mutters.
We look at each other till we both burp. He's from
another country, it's obvious when he speaks up:

"We just cut down every damn tree we need to
sell, end of discussion!" He'd touch you to your
very soul if he just looked at you, sweetly baby-
faced. "Go, son," I whisper, help him out the door.

ARROWS

Time, the mother of them all, she'd read.
What would you do if you knew it's real
purpose, George? Usually, it's good to
silence your tongue some too, his wife
said when Custer kissed her one last time.

The first one went through his hat. Who
knows how many more flew his way? We
know he stopped others from fleeing; you
can make a soldier out of most anyone.
What is it now, George? You can't avoid

starting at the first step if you hope to climb
any flights of stairs. Was Rousseau right, it's
useless relying on others? Even Steve Martin
was scared of the one through his silly hat.
How beautiful people sometimes are when

they're dying! Weren't we talking arrows a
while ago? Then, of course, there are bows,
bulls'-eyes, not to mention being outflanked.
What an eerie wistfulness about Sitting Bull
and Crazy Horse in the painting at the Frick.

So silent, just their eyes wander from one to
the other and back again, leaving nothing
to ponder but leaving this world, the utmost
whoosh of an arrow finding flesh. Reveling in
their emancipated state: quite a pang to it.

MACAK

Tesla's black cat, whose back I read
became a "sheet of light" when he

stroked it, the shower of sparks filling
the whole lab. "Is nature a gigantic

cat? If so, who strokes its back? Can
only be God," he said at last. Intended

for the clergy, which "prospect hung
like a dark cloud" on his mind, he'd

stretch himself like Macak, waiting for
the sun to show above the rim, its first

rays flashing across the horizon. Macak
came out from behind the stove, biting

into a tidbit Tesla held out till its nose
disappeared, very like Tesla in face,

the creature he most liked to be left
alone with, liked talking to when upset.

Some say he'd drop to a knee before
Macak, beg forgiveness, admit to being

foolish, but by and by come to his senses,
stop baying. "That's it," I hear him whisper

when Macak showers his face with licks,
"Be alone, that's the secret to inventing."

"BUSTER" (& PETER)

Courtesy of Houdini, who said,
"That was a real Buster!" when

young Keaton fell down a flight
of stairs. Also a stage-saying for

a spectacular pratfall, of which
Brecht was a particular fan who

wrote one into every production
he could, though Peter Lorre said,

"Not one in 'M' please!" Then all
grew dark and he staggered off

to lurk in more shadows till his
blood caught fire. Decline was

no longer out of the question:
witness what they did to him in

Hollywood, where he'd fled Nazis.
Brecht's greatest actor become

a sort of clown to Greenstreet's
menacing whimsies. Even Buster's

companionship couldn't keep
him from a short life, his melancholy

piggy-backing on Keaton's after
too many bottles of booze. "I must

try the world again," one or the other
mumbling, then giving into haunting

memories: troubled early times. No
use spoiling our lives thinking of them.

SLOW BOIL

Rocks rising in one place, sinking in another,
I read. Mostly quietly, inoffensively, almost
monotonously. Lots of history is as well, until
it's not of course. What are we to do, who

liked to eat and drink in peace, grass just
growing, flowers blooming? All seems quite
different now. We breathe more heavily, our
whole body working away, hands can't stop

waving, memories cropping up unaccountably.
Remember when we had our worst arguments
at recess, but quickly turned playful as puppies
in the snow, while our lower back goes out now

listening to TV news? Boiling over's not an option,
scrapes and bruises go septic, the doorbell rings,
an ambulance gurneys you off, doubts about
truths fester, the IV nurse smiling that grim way?

SENSITIVE PAPERS

Monod's favorite hiding place for them?
The giraffe, mounted with a hollow leg
outside his lab's door at the Sorbonne,
which the Gestapo never found. Inside,

his microscope bristled with E.coli cells,
but outside he'd just been appointed
Chief of French Resistance, having had
enough, he said, "of the enemy carting

off prisoners, killing our people, destroying
our dominions." Some said of Monod's ways,
"We don't know if it was a human or an
angel from God." Dark as thunder, head

bent, Monod's frowning in the tiny print
which hung on Gramma's wall, before
which she'd cross herself. "Saved many
a Jewish life too," her prayers ended on

Monod's mother's birthday. "She was
a Milwaukee girl, too; we sent her off
to Paris where Jacques was born, two
years before your mother," Gramma

said on her deathbed, to the end unable
to understand why I majored in German,
"the language of the enemy," instead of
pursuing a life in science like Jacques. "You

might have earned a Nobel Prize too, like
him," she said at last, her eyes dimming
under dark brows. It was not long after
I began to find fault with all my instincts.

INNOCENT GAZING

Crossing the Arabian Sea, D.H. Lawrence
lived out days of "unprecedented wonder,"

nowhere near nagging Frieda yet till final
bitterness set in; at peace with the empty

space before him, not expecting anyone
else to find fault with him. Where is that

drawing of him weaving a seine net, cutting
cords with his pocketknife, wattling them

with nimble fingers while watching waves
foam, break, then curl under? He seems to

be saying, "You can have one of my eyes,"
to the deckhand instructing him, whose

patch blackens his face. Whistler could
have painted them, but wouldn't have

called it "innocent gazing." Nor bowed his
head before it, as I had to without looking

up, till the museum guard said, "Closing
soon, sir." Wish I'd given him my copy of

Sons and Lovers; "But he must be made
abstract first," the only line underlined.

SULFUR PEARL

Biggest bacterium, have to dig in the mud
off the Namibian Coast to study it; the size
of a period, I read. Gram-negative, they'd

not make a pleasant necklace for someone
truly loved, who'd quickly ask for more water,
a little more bread till whispering, "Suddenly,

I can't seem to swallow." With a volume three
million more times than the average bacteria,
they'll grow even richer while she gets poorer.

You'll be left friendless, not to mention helpless,
see nothing but distress ahead. Meanwhile, for
scientists, since it was discovered in '97, things

are going along cheerfully, who follow paths
leading nowhere in particular at times, which
isn't the mother of all vices, while the rest of us

think to ourselves, Good Lord, why in heaven's
name did we go there, roll over, begin to perspire,
change the pillowcase, not a pearl of wisdom

in sight or mind. Best to move on to Namibia's
Diamond Coast, but if its stones aren't harmless
there's always Mercury Island farther out . . .

S CURVE

Aka sigmoid or logistic, said to be
the most important curve in the world.

Constant at first, its output increases slowly
with input so it seems constant, I read; but

watch out, it suddenly gets fast, then faster
till it gradually slows down to constant again.

Some scientists contend even gains and losses
affecting one's happiness follow an S curve.

Better hold my tongue some now, my brain's
turning inside out. Can't help wondering what

Darwin might think, knock on his study door: he's
in a chair by the window, cleaning his spectacles.

After I draw him some diagrams, sum up what
I've been reading, he puts his hands back of his

head. "My view is," he sort of stammers, "from a
purely theoretical standpoint it's probably absurd,

but from a practical standpoint quite a different
matter, which I leave to your century to work out."

With that he points to a magnum of rum left over
from the Beagle's voyages. I sleep faster the next

night, even faster the next, the future slowing down
to a trickle, almost nothing to it to arrest the heart.

SLOW, DUMB, TASTY

Says E.O. Wilson: A Basic Rule of Extinction.
Now I'll have it, it won't escape me, I thought
when I caught sight of its tail wrapping around

the highest branch of the coolibah tree where
we scattered Mom's and Dad's ashes another
lifetime ago. Had to rub my eyes, stop the urge

to blast away at a body up there belonging to
a creature crossing a human's path unlike any
I'd ever encountered. Especially in a desert I'd

been directed to by a friend's priest to think over
all I've said and done, starting with "the evil to self
when wishing harm to others." He'd waved off

a litany of misdeeds I wanted to recite, sketched
the trail up into the White Tank mountains where
he also loved to hunt before he took vows. "Still

oil my twelve-gauge lovingly," he confided, pushing
a chair out I fell into as if axed. That was mid April ; now
it's early September and it's clear there's little time for

"the waiting game"; so to an unknown fellow creature
high above I finally manage to say, "From this day on,
I'll try to live a quieter life, salute you for living yours."

THE STRAUB TAIL REACTION

"Inject a lab mouse with something
so its tail rises, arches over its back,
a classic case of opiate behavior!"
Dr. Holub said, introducing me to his
pet nude mouse that day we were
turned away from Kafka's grave by
a Russian tank crew on maneuvers
in the adjacent park, rudely escorted
back to Holub's clinic. "It's a good
thing we weren't caught helping
each other over the wall," he said.
We'd not been granted admission,
'who knows why?' a constant refrain
till the Velvet Curtain came down &
Havel promptly made Holub some sort
of science advisor. He didn't last, alas;
lost the struggle to change Havel's mind.

"BROWN COAL'S STILL OUR OPIATE!"
Holub's last postcard lamented, just
days before he dropped to the floor,
the razor still in his hand. No doubt one
of his many scientific papers centers
on the nature and cause of embolisms.

MINIMUM

The smallest size a warm-blooded animal
may be, e.g. the inch-long bumblebee,
the Etruscan pygmy shrew, who knew?

Whenever I roam around, hoping to add
to the list, all I discover has been already.
In the dark cellar weather I hang out in

lately, there's an occasional creepy-crawly,
a few spiders on their last legs, old torn webs
aplenty I vacuum up, happily no more mice

to chase, bats to net since insulating the Bilco.
But I'm one of the more cheerful octos you
might come across. My doc jokes he'd like to

sell my BP to his other oldies. My kids, looking to
book the London Palladium for my 100th, order
me to work up a routine, a la George Burns' . . .

Not taking that bait, sorry. Am more focused on
taking one step back to let the other damn fools
fall in first. Meanwhile, the marks on the wall will

tell you I'm shrinking more seriously now, so hurry
the science to undermine the inevitable, impede
the leaching melancholy known only to the old.

GOOGOLPLEX

First suggested, it's said, to be 1,
followed by writing zeros till you get
so tired there's some wine left.